ILLUMINATION

LEAVES
OF
MORYA'S
GARDEN

II

1925

Agni Yoga Society
319 West 107th Street
New York NY 10025
www.agniyoga.org

ILLUMINATION

1925

Welcome to seekers!

Welcome to bearers of the Common Weal!

Welcome of the East.

They will ask: "Who gave you the Teaching?"

Answer: "The Mahatma of the East."

They will ask: "Where does He live?"

Answer: "The abode of the Teacher not only cannot be made known but cannot even be uttered. Your question shows how far you are from the understanding of the Teaching. Even humanly you must realize how wrong your question is."

They will ask: "When can I be useful?"

Answer: "From this hour unto eternity."

"When should I prepare myself for labor?"

"Lose not an hour!"

"And when will the call come?"

"Even sleep vigilantly."

"How shall I work until this hour?"

"Enhancing the quality of labor."

One must manifest discipline of spirit; without it one cannot become free. To the slave discipline of spirit will be a prison; to the liberated one it will be a wondrous healing garden. So long as the discipline of spirit is as fetters the doors are closed, for in fetters one cannot ascend the steps.

One may understand the discipline of spirit as wings.

Whosoever will comprehend the discipline of spirit as illumination of the future worlds is already prepared.

He who has envisioned evolution will approach it carefully, joyously brushing away the dust on the path. Most important, there will be no fear in him. And rejecting the unnecessary he will acquire simplicity. It is easy to understand that the realization of evolution is always beautiful.

Again they will ask: "Why at the beginning of the path is so much that is pleasant accorded and so much forgiven?" It is because in the beginning all fires are full blown and the called one walks as a torch. It is up to him to choose the quality of his fire. He who comprehends the discipline of spirit will understand the direction of the fire and will approach the cooperation for the General Good. The end of the path can be illumined by a thousand fires of the General Good. These thousand fires will light the rainbow of the aura. Therefore, the discipline of spirit is wings!

1. Time was when even a hundred warriors were counted a host. Then a thousand were already an army.

In time a hundred thousand conquered the world. Afterwards millions rose but they also did not alter the orbit of the spirit. And so I shall summon under the Banner of Spirit one billion. This will be the sign of My army.

Consider when this manifestation will be fulfilled and seven banners will be affirmed!

2. The spirit is perfect only when it is conscious of the Cosmos. And it often happens, but we cannot always affirm ourselves in the realization of communion with the Truth.

The sky seems alive and we say, "Flies are swarming." Thus interpreted are finest touches of unseen wings.

The Void is the treasury of the Beginning, yet you feel the path of the Beginning.

3. Ponder each day how to fulfill My Work. Teach the inheritors—teach them beauty. Affirm their eye. Wherefore years, when one may accomplish in weeks?

It is easier to withstand a single roar than to permit thoughts to grow mouldy. Therefore, I say, let us proceed. Therefore I shall multiply your strength.

4. I shall send—fulfill My Will.

Cautiously contact the earthly. When one is on the way, delicacies are not needed.

5. For the inner work, let them sell the shield of lie.

6. I wish to speak of the pure and carefully passed karma.

Cautiously touch the tarred knots of destiny. It is much more dangerous to touch the already hardened past events, which are dragging after you. Therefore, I warn that the non-fulfillment of the decrees, disrespect of the Hierarchy, is more harmful that it seems.

The flow of karma can be covered by the ice of understanding. But beware of destroying this covering by foolishness or by cruelty, which is forbidden under Our Shield.

I repeat—guard the given path!

7. To whom shall we speak? A mule can draw a cart. Is it possible that the human spirit will not compel the body to rejoice in labor? The mule carries the rider to shelter in stormy weather. Is it possible that the human spirit is disturbed by the flow of karma?

8. The manifestation of the Teacher must be remembered; the Shield must be held in purity.

I will send all defense, I will send all possibilities, but hold the conduit firmly.

Amidst the maddened crowd veil the fire of the spirit. Read My book and be not terrified by the voices of calamities, for the blind do not perceive what is revealed to you.

But I say, for your benefit, evoke My Name more often. Do you deem it a pleasure to behold dead countries? But observe the downfall of the world of falsehood. Lie, lie, lie—perish!

9. The Teaching should be better understood. The Teaching should be applied resourcefully.

Smile at small stones!

10. The Teacher points out that you should learn to feel the bonds which have united you by the manifestation of miracles.

By a wondrous bast are your sandals tied for the long journey.

As was the past, so also will be laid the future.

One cannot have respite from predestined meetings.

And numberless are the sendings upon the pages of life.

Thus, all is prepared; but do not tear My web.

The whirlwind of folly blows away the best designs sent by Me. One should not strew about treasures which are bestowed for manifestation to the world.

Being a minor is not an excuse.

It is better to celebrate the victory after the first battle than to wander underground.

Therefore, I say, walk together and cover yourselves by one Shield. Let each one purify his breath without sprouting the dust of anger. And, gathering the flowers of devotion, you will understand the usefulness of My path.

Do I lead you by force? Compulsion is not Our ally.

But if we are walking together, why not give counsel! Therefore, I say to you, think better and do not stumble.

11. On Our scales the striving of the spirit is weightier than aught else. The success in life is strengthened only by the electricity of the prayer of achievement.

The teaching of spirit creates the armor of the body. Sensing the lightnings of the world, begin a new book for the coming winter.

I teach you to understand wisely the future. Success must follow My people.

You must wisely follow My milestones.

12. Sacrifice, sacrifice, sacrifice! Afterwards the receiving, and after that the triumph of the spirit.

13. Each one has his goal. I provide the gateway fitting for the spirit. Through it one may enter into

a transformed world, where the mind dwells at home in all lands.

The spirit learns to fly when sorrow sharpens the eyesight. The ray of realization of the Infinite illumines the bestowed good. There is the path of Earth and the path of wings. Discern and choose.

14. Clouds are gathering, but the Star of the Morning ascends.

15. Each moment of the spirit's understanding adds a gem to the treasury of possibilities.

16. Often through illness the achievements become intensified. St. Francis and St. Theresa were often ill. Pythagoras had heart disease. The best zurnas often lacked some strings.

17. Mothers, in their wisdom, foresee the occult conditions at the birth of a child. The mother's spirit knows how the enemy tries to harm the new wayfarer. During the transitory time of gestation it is easier to send the poison. It is easy to stir the mother's anger and to fill the home with the dust of discontent.

Mothers try wisely to direct their eyes toward the images of saints or to be comforted through the beauty of nature.

18. In giving we receive. Disdaining objects, we receive the heavenly raiment.

19. The form is animated by its contents and is not forgotten.

20. Daringly raise your shield. I ask one thing: not to weaken your strength with gold. My Teaching does not like gold.

21. There cannot be mercy when the law of Karma must be fulfilled up to the sign. Karma will overtake one, but its quality may be altered by a voluntary sacrifice to unknown people.

22. Sow better, sowers! Earth will soon be ready!

If he world is not helped by a special manifestation—Earth will not endure.

23. I shall call into My House those whom I see approaching.

The pending sword fills the spirit with pain.

24. Fulfill successfully the work that is pleasing to Me and advantageous to you, a friendly work which makes My House ready.

Gather the images of love. In love you will find the understanding of how better to adorn My House. Question your spirit as to what contents are befitting for My House.

Reverence will prompt one how to manifest the beauty of the clean House. The manifestation of your labor is like flowers. I shall take not an obol, but I will requite a hundredfold.

25. Even a simple housewife will say, "Do not soil the steps, or else you will have to clean them of your traces."

Similarly, those who pierce the aura of the Teacher and auras of those bound to Him harm themselves. There is not punishment, nor revenge, but there is the counter-spark.

Therefore, let them beware of touching Our Works, especially at present, when the electric force is tense.

Let it be said to those and to others who do not believe, "Better not touch; there may be thunder during sunshine."

But blessed are those who strengthen the armor of the aura.

26. Response can be given only to the pure in heart. Know how to combine the power of love with severity.

27. Welfare and health are found in trust. The necessary is always prepared by My Ray. Errors rend the tissue of the body.

28. One should not consider as a loss a concession to cunningly scheming hands.

The follower of wisdom likes to look far ahead. Stay the vile slanders by a smile bereft of irritation. The success of lightminded people is like the trickle of a small fountain, but a wise householder will labor to bring the water from the ocean and will then enjoy the eternal coolness of his fountain.

29. Cease speaking of enemies when an achievement can kindle a great light. Solitude will transmit the message better than the murmurs of crowds.

30. The world's basin is overflowing with bacilli. The web which covers it quivers. But the magic flower must be plucked on Earth by human hands.

I am with you, but when I become silent it means that I am receiving in My Shield arrows which are intended for you.

In unity, look toward the day of manifestation when knowledge will enter My House; for the carriers of knowledge are already born.

31. I speak of alien bridges and gates. On the way, alien bridges are encountered. One must cross them hurriedly, not looking downward, having but one wish—to reach quickly the other side. Also, do not pause before foreign gates, but demand the right of way without disturbing your calmness, because your way is determined. One must with pure thoughts close one's pores to bad air. But when times are difficult repeat: "Nevertheless, I am going into a Garden of Beauty. I fear not the predestined gates. Why is the shield above me? To safeguard me. If new dams arise I shall cross them, because I do not fear!"

32. Why merge into the astral world? Those rejoice who have suffered, who were aflame in spirit, and who labored. But here are the sowers and there the reapers.

A rich harvest manifests itself from all earthly seeds. The kernel sprouts; and likewise understanding masters the new dimensions of future seeds. Therefore, why question the astral world?

33. Now, about the messenger: Even as in life one hastens to meet the postman, in the same way must one stretch out one's hand towards Our sending. A front of barbed obstacles impedes Our messengers, but you have miraculous shears for cutting the obstructions. By keeping the aura clear help the messengers to reach you.

It is difficult for a dove to fly in the fog. I lead you by the speediest path and at the moment of obscuration I am ready to send a messenger. But open the doors to him; it is difficult to stand knocking in the rain.

Love the solitude of thought, when the sparks of understanding weave a wreath of knowledge. And as I have vouched for you, so entrust yourselves to Me. With the Hand of Power I affirm the path to the Heights. Apprehend the Good when My Envoys will bring the tidings: "He has come!" The hour of happiness is ordained, and on the way there are flowers.

What do the far-reaching hands, dogs and tigers matter to you? Perform the great task of the living God.

34. The meaning will be clear when you will look from the mountain tops. One must observe the sparks; soon they will begin to merge into the flame of a new understanding of the foundations.

To build an arch between the ways of the full decline and the ascent is not easy. The carriers of spirit do not recognize each other. Harken to and record the voices of strange figures on your way. Afterwards you will weld together these informations, thus revealing the ladder of practical possibilities.

The knife of attention is sharpened, the bond gets

stronger, and skillful sparks alert your power without infringing upon karma.

35. I shall explain why it is important to heed the words and the given images. Our pupils have an exercise of thought in which out of a whole message a part or a single word is given and, perceiving the direction of the thought, each one adds to it according to his understanding, sensing that which is closest to himself. But in time the personal is superseded by a united consciousness, and upon a single word there is built a complex structure. Thus is attained the code of spirit.

36. Occultly, the circle appears as an impersonation of the human organism broadened by possibilities.

The central figures carry the honorary functions of the heart. The growth of the organism and its injuries are reflected upon the heart. The waving of the arms calls forth fatigue and, furthermore, the non-realization of strivings. You already know the parable about the ring-dance and about the shields. You already know that the best number for the circle is seven. Five represents the extremities of the body. Supplements can carry only special functions or else the acquittal of a karmic condition.

It is difficult to form a circle, but it is still more difficult to make substitutions; because one cannot replace the heart by an extremity and it is impossible to introduce an undisciplined spirit. For such cases there are witnesses near at hand who will not burden the artery of a heart far away.

37. Now, about karma.

If to the realized burden be added the bonds of karma, then how hard it becomes to carry the whole unorganized thinking. One can alleviate this by cautiously avoiding contact with the nerve perceptions. But human thinking so easily unbalances the scales, only to throw off its weight, which drags one earthward.

But for each such gesture of the hand the poor heart aches.

38. It is a difficult task not to add enemies. One should be aware of the stones at the threshold but one should not be distressed by them.

39. Not one, not two, but a multitude of hearts have been directed to you, and the net of possibilities is being woven by skillful hands. But do not tear the net. Pay attention to the manifestation of each day.

Luxury must leave you. You will assume a distinct appearance, and you will find it in conformity with the nature of My country.

To the utmost limits of brain must you be immersed in the realization of My possibilities. It does not befit anyone to become wearied.

40. The gnats are displeased with the breeze; they cannot reach you nor sting you.

Do not make new enemies. They who are ordained for you will themselves come.

41. Only the harmony of the battery can control the power. The Ray can manifest its significance only when you act in accordance with Decree.

42. When you will speak in My Name, say: "The Hand of the Creator is always in motion; therefore, all is moving." You see upon your ring two spirals. As upon one one may ascend, so upon the other one may descend. Even an Arhat can descend, by misuse of miracle.

Be steadfast not only during the time of Communion with Me, but also when you are left to your own devices, because only then is the resourcefulness of the spirit forged.

When they will suspect you of love for Us, you will be vindicated by My Shield.

I shall send you seven opportunities to manifest resourcefulness. Many window panes may be broken, and uncomfortable is the house with such apertures.

By the Will of the Hierarchy you can preserve the entrusted treasure.

Gird yourself with a determined desire and, looking at the ring, repeat, "I will not descend!"

43. Consider exultation as a powerful manifestation on the way to Us.

The old is for the old ones. My Sign should be preserved in a new book, with a new spirit, through new action.

44. When the raindrop taps upon the window—
    it is My Sign!
When the bird flutters—
    it is My Sign!
When the leaves are borne aloft by the whirlwind—
    it is My Sign!
When the ice is melted by the sun—
    it is My Sign!
When the waves wash away the sorrow of the soul—
    it is My Sign!
When the wing of illumination touches the harried
    soul—it is My Sign!

Count the steps when you approach the Temple, because each seventh step carries My Sign!

When you will manifest a new understanding of My Sign, you will perceive the flash of the Worlds' lightning. I have opened the door to you, but only by yourself may you enter it.

45. I say irrevocably: While with Me, while without irritation, while without doubt, the streams of possibilities are incalculable.

Unutterable are the Forces which serve you. They who carry the Stone radiate the stars of benevolence.

New possibilities are given each day. Weave baskets in which to gather these stars. Spread the linen of the tents to catch the gifts, for thus I lead you!

46. Labor in the morning hours; in the evening rejoice in My Name. I bid you on a new way!

47. My Ray—thy breath.

> My Hand—thy banner.
> My Shield—thy pride.
> My House—thy refuge.
> My Mountains—thy marvel.
> My Wish—thy law.
> My Manifestation—thy happiness.

May the spirit of Our Brotherhood abide with you.

48. Penetrating, through the Teaching, into the essence of the happiness bestowed, one must walk with firm tread, confident of resurrection of the greatest hope of humanity, based upon the Stone.

Let us in prayer await our destiny.

49. Vicious voices are trying to spread dust. But remember that irritations are no better than dust, and avoid them. I teach through the manifestations of life. I give daily signs. As rose petals are strewn the signs, for the time is near. Think of the New World; think of the procession of peoples.

50. I repay a hundredfold, but what is lost retards one a hundredfold.

O ball of destiny! Where wilt thou fall and whither rebound? The Light has been revealed to thee. Succeed, thou ball, in reaching it in time! Restrain thy evil cunning whirl.

51. When you will stand at the wailing wall remember that joy is coming!

To you I say it! Turn to the East, behold My Dawn! Beauteous is the chrism stored up in time! Precious is the flower planted in My Hour! Do not spill the chalice of My Hour! The Miracle comes!

Accept your heritage, waiting ones! The vessel of ancient times has returned!

52. Why do you marvel at the given dates? We do not guess—We see.

You will ask how you should gather. I will tell you to gather in prayer. Better be silent, without the clatter of objects, without the raising of voices, because the wings of spirit grow in quiet. Dedicate in prayer the time of Our Communions, because for the Communion We shall bring the very best. The current of Communion creates a wondrous ladder to the very loftiest manifestations of the Creator—the ladder of Spirit. You can struggle in life, you can discern when is the hour to invoke My Hand.

53. How to await the development of works? As waves have their rhythm, so do the works grow: in measured rising and expectant flowing progression. Understand the hour of the clarion; heed the pace of life.

In moments of silence store up the teaching on the shelf of experience.

How should one read the writings of the Wise Ones? One must isolate oneself and apply what is read to one's different moods.

Here am I, newborn.

Here am I, an old man.

Here am I, an exile.

Here am I, a sovereign.

Here am I, blind.

Here am I, one who has cognized worlds.

To all sources apply all the conceivable greatness of the Lotus.

54. One should not hesitate. Walk like lions! Righteousness adorns your armor.

I will reveal Myself to you as an angler, and I will thrust My Hand into the wheel of threats. I say that one should learn by the examples of attack. The fire of Earth wants to break through.

My command to disciples, and lawful is My request, is to walk sternly but without irritation. Irritation makes one's vessel crystalline and fragile. A silver chalice better befits the Stone. I check the shower of small arrows. Now the time is so near when the ancient pledge will be fulfilled.

55. By spirit retain the spiritual Teaching; only spirit can bring the Kingdom of God onto the Earth. As simply as My Words will the Kingdom of Spirit approach. As simply as last winter's dry leaves will be swept away.

There is no past, there is the light of the future—by it walk! I summoned you from the gulf of life. I sharpened your teeth. I set before you the color of the banner. Understand the Teaching with a full sweep of wings. To Me leads only the upper path; by the lowest path one cannot come. Hold My Commandments under sagacious locks. Ascend by the most valiant thoughts, for I have lifted the flap of your tent with lightning. In spirit forget about insignificance. The predestined Light is great. So walk!

56. Pure thoughts are obstructed by gratuitous judgments of local people. It is difficult to hear behind the forest. In the works you love, My laws must be defended.

57. I want to tell you to proceed more boldly, with all the power of spirit. The fetters of Earth will not impede you. Success will accompany the courageous ones.

As mountain flowers find it hard to pass even one night in a swamp, so for you it is not easy. The enemy's stroke sounds upon the strings, but claws cannot compose a symphony.

Many darts has My Shield diverted from you.

58. It is easy to dig a ditch, but difficult to erect a house. Hostile scoffing fills the corners with dust. But with a feather of the wing you will wipe away the dust. Therefore, guard the wing.

59. My Sign can lead you. Keep My House in mind. Only thus will you attain.

Your destiny is to avoid crowds, sending them the highest Good.

Pure is the mountain's silver, but one must find the way to it. But the dirt of these days is as naught in the light of the future.

One can understand people's wearisome thought when one peers into human breath; like smoke it clouds the air. The suffering is transmitted on the waves of the ether.

Not sooner than the predestined date must the Earth break the chain forged by men.

60. Great is the light given by Our Teaching.

Only the new to the new ones.

61. To create a wave of power, it suffices to have faith in the signs. Thus, mutually we help the manifestation of light.

Carry within your inmost self the marvelous, enlightened thought—to see Our House.

When you feel the manifestation of an achievement, then remember that a wondrous thread is incandescing. My Soul rejoices to realize that none will stop you. I am sending you joy; show attention. Manifest calmness; the convulsion will end.

62. The judgment of the lightminded revolves like

a wheel. A daring one asks for a bow; he will fetch the bird himself.

63. Success should be nursed as a flower.

64. My Eye—your light
My Hand—your defense.
My Heart—your anchor.

One love holds the thread of the spirit's achievement. The gulf will not swallow the fire.

65. Forward flies the shot—there is no turning back.

66. Success manifests wings. Seekers of achievement, I will safeguard you upon the wave's crest and set you above a precipice as on an inaccessible tower.

67. Desiring evil for others, they are themselves extinguished. Dark are the times. Hold firmly the Shield. As water sprayed, so will be scattered they who retreat.

68. Show a firm pace. Guard the heart, because a vessel which contains the whole world must be cautiously borne. Simply walk forward without wincing. Withholding irritation, you create a new sheath for the spirit. Even a steed gallops better when not frothing.

69. As sparks create ozone, so the work of the spirit weaves assistance. Just open a clean window and help flies in.

70. Invisible teaching proceeds unceasingly. The distinction of the spirit is cognized only on the boundaries of the steps. The growth of the spirit is marked by an invisible thermometer.

71. Courage must be gathered to pass like lions—thus grows an achievement. Do not bewail the past but be ready to raise the shield at any hour.

72. For all I enjoin courage. Even a dove should become a lion. Not We but you are in need of your courage. With a smile arrest the destruction of the temple. Only by courage can you master a flight. All will

happen in due time. Understand that one must repeat: "Courage and patience." Let people look at the task of polishing a stone: how firmly and cautiously moves the workman's hand—and only for his daily pay. Incomparable is the work of a creator.

73. Knowledge comes only with the readiness of the spirit. Commanding and terrorizing are only for the enemies.

74. I will bestow on each according to his merit. The greater contributor will receive the more. I will reward every self-sacrifice. I will tame all forgetfulness. I will give joy!

Let him whom the fiery way is dangerous freeze with cockroaches.

Be satisfied with the flow of wondrous Benevolence, for hail strikes painfully. It is better to receive My Ray.

75. Who follows the New World will receive a silver staff.

76. I avow that everyone and everything is tested. Who will be unafraid to rise to Us?

77. We can give a thread, but you must sharpen the needle. Material is given, but you must pierce it yourself. Walk the loftiest path.

The sail should be snow-white.

78. Through fire, through smoke, through miracles, through faith—walk!

Sparkle with youth of spirit; be most young and mobile. The sail of achievement is most lasting.

79. Only exultation of spirit enables one to cross the radiant bridge. I sow tokens—gather them resourcefully.

80. Your power will grow, but if you smother the flame you will burn your hands. Let the flame of faith shine freely. The Teacher watches each thought, ready to select the best seeds of the spirit.

81. M∴ and the understanding of Buddha's Teaching lead one to the vital understanding of law, conceived upon the Mount of Light. His Law will be of much help on the way to knowledge. His Teaching is My joy. My Hand leads to knowledge.

Smile when spiritual beggars are called scholars. Smile when someone speaks irreverently about the spirit's understanding, when false books are read, when pure thoughts frighten the small of soul.

82. Learn to consider a Decree immutable.

You will marvel when the waves of people will raise the pledge of ancient times.

83. Ailments of the spirit are as contagious as those of the body. This is a simple scientific consideration. Strike upon a table and the objects will vibrate. So much more does a spiritual blow shake the nerves.

You may touch old things and consciously expel the harm of accumulations.

84. In love forge the affirmation of the Heights about the ability to control oneself. My Teaching cannot be belittled by the foolishness of hostile slanderers. I see they will badly bruise their brows; but give them time.

When we approach the Commandment of Christ and Buddha, what is the dust of the threshold to us? An oyster shell without its contents.

85. Display speed. Spilled seeds are difficult to gather.

86. Learn to comprehend the manifestation of the Teaching as a miracle, in order to manifest the shield on all paths. I feel each moment that is useful to you.

Our Front Line stands as a wall, and a smile flashes as lightning over all faces at each of your successful moves. As a gardener sees that the garden be covered with buds, uprooting the weeds, so We watch the movements of the chosen hands. Joyous is each resourcefulness, because the shield is forged on both sides. Broad is My Work; to everyone a place ordained. By the broadness of your vision will you allot your own part. The manifestation of unprecedented possibilities is behind the door. Give Us reason to rejoice!

87. It is good to be in the sunshine, but the star-lit sky also brings harmony to the nerves. The moon, on the contrary, is not for us. The moon's pure light affects the prana. The magnetism of the moon is great, but for repose it is not good. Often the moon evokes fatigue, like people who devour one's vital energy. The manifestation of miraculous power increases during moonlight.

A pure prana must respond to the attraction, otherwise there is no miracle but a destruction of the vital treasure trove. While resting it is good to laugh, for the thyroid gland is purified by laughter. To purify the glands is a primary duty.

88. Shambhala is the indispensable site where the spiritual world unites with the material one. As in a magnet there exists the point of utmost attraction, so the gates of the spiritual world open into the Mountain Dwelling. The manifested height of Guarisankar helps the magnetic current. Jacob's Ladder is the symbol of Our Abode.

89. Superstition can be driven out only by respecting the forces innate in man.

One must know how people are awaiting My Coming. People's desire forges a new rung for the ladder.

90. The density of matter obstructs each experiment of the spirit. This concerns men as well as the whole of nature. For access to it matter must be melted. In the process of smelting there is produced a specific gas which assimilates with the substance of the

spirit. In man, a gas emanates from the nerve centers at each ecstasy of happiness or unhappiness. Thus a laboratory of the spirit is obtained. Therefore, a misfortune is called the visitation of God, but each somnolent existence is death of spirit. In nature, ecstasies manifest as thunder-storms, earthquakes, eruptions of volcanoes and floods. A similar laboratory of spirit begins to work. Hence, all sparks of ecstasy are blessed. Molten matter yields to improvement and provides new formulae. Instead of prolonged researches it suffices to reflect the elements in Our mirrors, and then to accumulate new formulae. Then remains the second part of the work: patiently, and in due time, to give them to people. Upon the fires of ecstasy travels Our Ray, seeking admittance into the heart. Where is the happiness or misfortune that has opened the entry? But, contacting molten matter, one senses the pulse of Earth, and the heart must withstand the gravitation. Those who will take part in this work must guard their hearts. Therefore, I say, guard the heart—all else is easy to repair. It represents matter, whereas the nerves are subservient to the spirit. At the knock of the spirit the door of the solar plexus is opened. But each stroke of matter beats upon the heart. Whoso- ever wishes to come in touch with the formula of matter must guard the heart. Our medicine teaches how to strengthen the heart through breathing; but about this another time.

91. The nerve emanation is imponderable; it is odorless and invisible, because it is of the spirit. The product of the heart is blood, with all its earthly dimensions. Therefore, when it is said that one must feel with the heart, this means it should be adapted to the earthly plane.

The sole bridge between the spirit's understanding and the embracement of the earthly plane is the white blood corpuscle. But you know what conflict attends their existence. Do not the white corpuscles, subject to the forces of Earth and bearing the knowledge of spirit, seem to you like White Brothers? This is why harmony is so difficult on Earth. But to work there where the spirit has descended into matter, the conditions of both planes must be met. One should not estrange oneself from the earthly, yet one must abide in spirit. For the mastery of the earthly formulae, one must possess a strong channel of the heart, because the reflex of the earthly signs carries dangerous sparks. But for Earth, all must be accomplished upon the earthly plane. Therein is the chief reason for the existence of the Brotherhood here. Therefore, upon Earth one must reach Us, discover Us, as silver ore—the best beneath the earthly crust.

92. At present great understanding of the revelation of the highest Teaching takes place.

It is good to understand that the possession of objects should be devoid of a feeling of property ownership. It is good to possess things in order to take care of them, and even to surround them with a benevolent aura, with the thought of passing them on to others. The manifestation of a creative hand dwells in a house whose occupants are without attachment to property, and being improved it will carry joy further. The sign of the bestowing hand will be preserved continuously, and therein lies the justification of objects. Through this understanding is solved the most difficult problem. I say this for the world, because the ruination of the world arises chiefly from attachment to non-existent property. To inculcate this in the new people means to cure them of the fear of old age. Possession devoid of the sense of ownership will open the path to all without conventional inheritance. Who can improve, shall possess. This concerns lands, forests and waters. All mechanical achievements and various types of inventions are subject to the same principle. It is easy to imagine how folk creation will begin to work, especially in the knowledge that only the spirit offers the best solution. To the hearth of spirit shall be directed questions as to how best; and the sword of the spirit shall strike any evil guile. Verily, it is profitable to do better. The law is simple, as is everything of spirit.

93. Events have so piled up that the organisms of sensitive people are in tremor. One must ascribe the tremor of nerves to Cosmic disturbances. Nothing should be exposed under a shower, but afterwards the sun is especially radiant.

94. Monetary alms should be abolished, as help can be provided through labor or objects. There will be none without work when people will turn to the path of spirit. We intend to demonstrate this advantage of perfectionment not for the invisible world but for you yourselves. We summon to Our Path.

95. Assemble the most unfortunate ones, the most obscure young students, and reveal to them the gift of power to endow humanity. Advise them to write the statutes in the Temple. It is long since the world has witnessed assemblages in the Temple. Christ will bestow His Grace upon the attaining ones. We wish to see the Temple beautiful and alive. And no one shall expel those walking to Light, for ruin awaits him. Miracles will be received upon the tablets of knowledge.

Let each one who is illumined by spirit walk boldly into the Temple. Our Path leads to the transformation of Earth into a palace. There are no poor. Who is unwilling to accept riches?

96. I rejoice to see how you understand the details of My Decrees. I prepare an event, foreseeing all details.

Act likewise, as thus it will be easier for us to meet each other.

One should not scatter to the winds a part of what has been predestined. Being resourceful, one need not deviate from the path. Intense attention is important. A vigilant spirit walks ahead of understanding. My Ray is ready to kindle the lightning flash of thought.

And thus shall we pass between all dangers; and failure will turn into success.

97. Maitreya sends courage. Maitreya will accept the gift. Maitreya feels its love. Maitreya sends blessings upon the joyous labor. Maitreya bestows labor upon Earth in the name of miracle. Walk joyfully. It is a joy to Me to lead the smiling ones. Discern the Teaching of Light in each manifestation. Resourcefulness is a quality of My pupils.

98. I enjoin you to behold a miracle needed to peoples. You will know how to reach the hearts of men.

As the arm can move only from the shoulder, so does the consciousness move from the brain. One must detonate the brain; then the consciousness is projected forward as from a cannon.

The Teaching flies upon the wings of events. Say: "I may wait today, because, though tomorrow shall follow even without me, meanwhile I can strengthen myself." How can one advise when and what rubbish should be sold on the market? We shall not display ourselves when we put on new garments. Let them believe there is nothing to put on. Even the keys of the trunks must not rattle. We shall draw the curtains of the windows.

99. The law of the transition into the spirit world is not complex. The one condition may not be likened to the other. As the dust of a volcano, so countless are the spirits who return to the spiritual world. Of course,

32

matter is a condition of spirit. But blood differs so greatly from its equivalent in the spirit, which is nurtured by prana, that the boundaries are broken throughout all Worlds. It is with difficulty that the spirit realizes its release from matter. The spirit attached to Earth clothes itself in the astral body, which creates for him the illusion of Earth here in the hearth of cravings and remorse. But the spirit which speeds out, in upward striving only, can avoid the astral plane, because the astral body is but superfluous rubbish. The less litter the purer the consciousness. On Earth it is difficult to conceive of forsaking matter without despising it, abandoning it for a new formation. But you have the best example in the giving away of any objects. The best donor will devise the best gift. Therefore, the matter which has garbed a lofty spirit affords the greater usefulness because nothing is wasted. Of course, a conscious communion is accessible to lofty spirits if the appeal is sufficiently freed from questions of matter and blood. The spirit, nurtured by prana, does not assimilate blood. Therefore, one may divide the world on the basis of blood; no other demarcation exists.

The seed of the spirit continuously carries life on, and the balloon of nerve emanations caries the spirit into the heights the spirit has determined. Therefore, to speak of immortality as of a purely scientific fact is profoundly correct. Upon the casting away of matter, the final thought is like an arrow. This moment determines the direction of the flight; the rest is added according to the aspiration. Let us know how to aspire. Let us construct a rainbow conjoining the steps of the spirit's ascent.

100. Let us speak of death.

Death is no more than the shearing of the hair, for in the same way is matter cast off. The question of Guides is answered by the familiar law of attraction and repulsion. The principle of requitement and assistance is a powerful one in the spiritual world. Therefore, every appeal of an embodied spirit evokes a response. It depends upon who asks. One can attract and keep near oneself lofty forces. Also, the lowest spirits may be fastened about oneself. One receives what one wishes. When men understand the usefulness of pure giving, they will receive riches.

The spirit is a light of the beauty of the stars. But few spirits blend with light; more of them are in astral bodies. Better to glow as a star, retaining knowledge and the possibility of returning to the planets to help. One may choose a better destiny—are the possibilities of the giving one not evident?

One may strive upwards toward light, seeking to render assistance; then there is no parting. If those who remain would consider the departed as having been sent to light and for enlightenment, then the communion would be more sound. The loftier the spirit, the more he beholds—it depends upon the development of the spirit. A lofty spirit feels whither to strive—it flies as an arrow. But a dark one hovers behind the stove. Therefore, precious is the bold desire to seek, because he who seeks finds. If the desires of the spirit are lofty it can discover lofty forms, and in creating them it can contribute to perfectionment.

101. The law of the saturation of space is similar to that of cementation. Legends, prophecies and manifold signs have major significance not for the separate individuals but for the cementing of space. Our communions reveal the book of the growth of the spirit's understanding. Not by the way of miracle but by that of daily routine do We work. I vouch that even from spawn one can learn. Each ovum of the spawn bears a

complete organism. Thus, a many-hued sac of thought imbues space.

102. A cloud is no miracle; meanness is not achievement; ruination is not cleverness. But the awakened spirit grasps understanding immediately. Therefore the Brotherhood has abnegated the manifestation of miracles. Signs can accompany events only as banners. One should discard miracles as a means of persuasion, because miracles have never convinced. Some speak of a personal communion; but the air is for all, although many do not wish to understand its use—precisely its use.

New strivings may be born over the graves of old prejudices—one more conquest. I have already told you of the spirit understanding. When the Ray unites the Teacher with the disciple, then the main understanding is transmitted by the spirit's perception. Not letter, not sign, but infallible spirit knowledge guides the conduct of the disciple. This infallible knowledge is the speediest conduit. Actually it is not a matter of mental decision, it is spirit-knowledge.

I am sending you arrows of simple attainments. Not to all is the simplest path accessible, but if you can understand—good for you.

103. And the call of the Mother is heard! Not by magic but in spirit shall you attain. Can magic affirm the Stone? Nor can people become affirmed through magic. But when each one understands that the spirit's way is simple, and brings the call of the Mother of the World, then each one will find the Gates open.

Without lamentations and invocations each one may approach the apparatus of life—not through mind but in spirit. The hands will be stretched out not to entreat but to gather. The call of the Mother will show the Gates whereby it is already time to enter. Just the

Call of the Mother. When the whims of childhood are forgotten, only Mother can call.

The repast is ready. The hour is come when a new feast is spread. Approach, while the dishes are still hot! Many will not be able to swallow the hot food; but the boldest one, like the fairy tale prince, will swallow the fire of the world. And the path of fire will illumine the nearest road.

104. Our thoughts are about you. We are sending you the Teaching—how to walk upon the steep rock, transforming it into a wondrous valley. Humanity feels that the solution is not to be found by the sword, and the last possibility sent is the indication of the Gates.

Success is only a sign of the correct direction. Success is but the understanding of the moment. The Teaching is but the lifting of the curtain of the theater. How wonderful it is to be an actor in the world's mystery! Walk in joy! The unbroken chain has great value. My Hand sends rays from the mountains. We shall begin the New Era without delay. I teach not to dream but to harken to the flow of events.

105. Contemplate memory and consciousness.

Since memory is for the past, consciousness is for the future. Therefore We replace memory by consciousness. By means of memory I cannot penetrate within the boundaries of the sun, but consciousness opens the gates. For Us, the museum and library replace the memory; therefore, disciples should not grieve over the loss of the old memory. It is simply that a small thing is replaced by a great one. Consciousness is akin to the spirit understanding; it grows until one's whole being is engulfed as in a flame. During this process the chips of memory, like dross, impede the burning. To know does not mean to remember. He who attains hastens on without looking back.

Humanity must remember the transmutation of consciousness.

Wherein lies the strength of Our experiments? In the solar consciousness, being poured out as prana. Above the stratum of earthly thoughts stream the currents of the sun's wisdom, and in these regions begins the great preordained Teaching. We summon to the encompassment of the Universe. But only the instrument of consciousness will permit the new experiments of the blending of spirit and matter.

Karma cannot complicate a harmonious body.

Therefore, the path of ascent is of practical benefit.

106. Beyond the roots of eternal Truth there is much dust. The time has come to remove excrescences.

107. My Book must be understood better. The Teaching of how to walk upon Earth is revealed to those who consider heaven to be alive. A teacher is one who can walk firmly upon Earth. I repeat that there should not be renunciation of earthly life without full understanding of its manifestation. One should understand with sensitiveness the events of each day. When the date strikes, even an ant may come as a messenger.

108. Merging into the summits of Cosmos, one must find coordination with Earth. Each moment We are ready to forsake everything of Earth and at the same time We love every blossom on it. Therein lies the wisdom as to what remembrance to cherish: whether about the crown or the fragrance of freezias, the shouts of victory or the songs of shepherds. That which is the most dear but least of all belonging to us is the best load to carry on the way. Song brings us health, and blossoms will heal wounds. Therefore, I say, happy are those who understand sound and color.

From the very beginning the prophets have noted sound and color. The ancient instruction about the ringing of bells is full of meaning. Wreaths and garlands recall the understanding of healing power. According to the color of his radiation, each one is attracted by flowers. White and lilac have affinity with the purple, blue with the blue; therefore, I advise to keep more of these colors in the room. One can follow this in living flowers. Plants wisely selected according to color are more healing. I advise to have more freesias. Our Ray, with its silveriness, is more reminiscent of white flowers. Color and sound are Our best repast.

109. A whirlwind evoked by crimes stifles the hoary Earth. Fumes float about, obscuring the mind. The iron shower is beyond endurance. One should be cautious. Beware—success lies not in haste but in the understanding of the times. The hand of fate leads toward the inevitable dates. Desire the manifestation of the New World. It is not We who shake the empires; We only sweep away the decay. It is important to understand the rhythm of the tide: now the lofty joy of understanding, now destruction.

110. Not treatises, not logic, but the channel of spirit brings the perception of Cosmos. The tenor of contemporary life has severed from humanity all understanding of the universal power. The perspicacity to penetrate the superterranean spheres is manifested only at the boundary line of sleep. He who can appreciate this sacred moment has already begun to lift the veil. Not visions but consciousness is important. Not what is compelled by training but what results from voluntary revelation is valuable.

The approaching time must put at the disposal of every sensitive spirit the tripod of Pythia. A kind of democratization of the features of aristocracy. But everyone inescapably bears in his bosom scales impossible to cheat. Each one will allot himself immediately what he deserves. This conforms with the New Era and easily reaches people's psychology. Understanding the flow of people's thought, it is easy to foresee the consequences.

111. Know how to turn the thrusts to advantage. Desire many enemies, but do not make them.

Let us conclude that begun yesterday: the recompensing for bad and good actions must be accelerated. The primary concern of religion should be to provide a practical solution to life. The heavenly reward is too remote; the return should be brought within the earthly span. People can now understand as universally accessible the miracle of the renewal of possibilities. Hence, either the hand of the Invisible Friend or a sharp sword. And, remembering the advantage of immediate remuneration, people will find a new path to the Temple. There is no need to implore Divinity. One should bring to oneself the best deed.

112. The greatness of Cosmos precludes scrutiny; it overwhelms and exalts. Spirit-knowledge is cognized by the spirit's knowledge. Pay attention to the silvery thread that connects one in spirit with the spirit of the Guide and extends its silvery manifestation up to the Ruler of the Planet. There results a network of conduits from the Supreme Spirit. The highest individualization does not fear union, and the gifts of revelation are sent along the silvery thread up to the highest spheres. Similarly, at the birth of a spirit a lofty Spirit sends him his conduit.

Remember, every kind of occurrence is possible in the world of spirit. New possibilities are molded not by an invented formula but by an indescribable power of spirit. It is both difficult and wonderful.

113. I rejoice at your prophetic possibilities for only through them can the best evolution in the future be

secured. Knowledge of the past without foresight does not lead onward.

114. The purification of religions predicates a new direct relation with the spiritual world. Christ, Buddha and their closest coworkers did not use magic formulae but acted and created in full blending with the spirit. Therefore, in the new evolution the former artificial methods must be abandoned. Remember cause and effect. The mechanics of yogism are no longer suitable for the regeneration of the world. A teacher who sits under a tree and forbids does not conform to the need.

Whence does one derive strength and wisdom? In union with the Great Spirit, recognizing cause and motive, we build an immediate consequence. We evoke Those who earlier did set out on the great path of personal realization and responsibility. And our appeals, through thousands of raised hands, reach Them. There is no need to implore, no need of terror, but unity moves masses. Desiring the good, we accept the heritage of the Great Carriers of good. We leave our spiritual vessel open for reception of beneficences. Nothing of evil will touch us, for we desire only that good which has been affirmed by the spirit. And carefully shall we deliver the web of writings into the treasury, because we are going to the Sources.

To be prepared, to be self-denying, to be abused, to be calumniated, to be joyful, to be silent, to be jubilant, to be the bringing and the bestowing one, and to be in this life taught by the light of the sun, is to be as We wish to see you; and as such We are dispatching you. Thus has your spirit accepted the mission.

Not with a royal domain, not out of the alchemist's cellar, not with conjurations of magic, but in the midst of life, do we go and come to You, our Elder Brothers and Sisters, to receive the treasures preserved by You, accumulated by us, because we go into the simple Temple of the Supreme Spirit. Thus we shall return to You, because thus do You wish to see us; and the load imposed by You we shall safeguard as the Chalice of Immortality.

115. Not by accident do bits of the luminaries reach neighboring spheres. They are like a means of communication. These signs are neglected by modern science. The importance does not lie in that an aerolite may contain carats of diamonds, but in its significance as a psychomagnet. By this means men can enlarge the sphere of communication. In the future coordination of matter, this quality of psychomagnetism is important; because matter must finally blend with spirit, must become fusible, like glass. Towards the beginning of the new step of evolution a new means of healing may be applied by grouping people according to the rays of the luminaries. To go beyond the confines of the planet is the immediate objective. Not a spectator of the worlds is man, but a conscious coworker; and his way lies not through puddles, but through the radiance of the spheres.

Why search for Light when one should sense it? The spirit knows it is accessible to him and predestined for him. Otherwise, wherefore the ladder of Our Brotherhood? It rests on the earth and has merged with the heavenly spheres.

116. Courageously withstand the dreadful attacks. Your spirit must rejoice at each action. While the hens cackle, the rain comes and the harvest is good. In the barn is much dust, but from the barn comes bread.

117. There is power in repetition. Although incorrectly applied in religion, in life this armor is indispensable. One must repeatedly enwrap oneself.

118. "Whoever succeeds in hearing the voice of

his spirit will rise above the precipice." Thus spoke Saint Sergius. "He who has retired into the woods cannot hear the talk of people, and he who then falls asleep will not hear the birds—heralds of the Sun. And he who is reticent at an evident miracle will relinquish his sight. And he who is hesitant about helping his brother will not draw the splinter from his own foot." Thus spoke Saint Sergius.

Of Sergius one will have to speak; people will want to know about Him. Thus, We shall throw color upon the Image of St. Sergius, illumining in narration His life and sayings.

119. Let us speak of the auras.

The egg-shaped aura is natural to the astral body. The most usual, the narrow aura, which emanates from the entire body, extends outward about two inches. In accordance with the degree of spirituality, it begins to expand from the upper nerve centers. Starting from the solar plexus, it afterwards rises toward the brain centers, forming the so-called solar aura. Influxes of blood are characteristic of the transposition of the aura, when the current of tension shifts its pressure. Even fainting spells are possible. Finally, the radiation leaves the lower extremities and forms a surrounding ring. The organism while yet in the midst of life becomes acutely sensitive, especially to sounds and colors. The utmost tranquility is needed during this transitory period. The solar aura may be of ten or fifteen inches, and of course its dimensions may increase.

In spite of the discomfort of transposition of the aura, one may congratulate him who has acquired the upper radiation. The opportunity for repose should be cautiously created. Later on a seeming new armor grows, as the nerves of the skin become strengthened. One cannot exactly divide the physical and the spiritual. The balance fluctuates and the waves travel over the organism. This must not be called a malady, but the organism must be assisted every moment to fortify itself in its new condition.

120. As you felt loneliness before, so now you must feel the spirit-knowledge. There is bidding to each new step. Permit volition to the spirit. Exercise caution, in conformity with the spiritual consciousness. Ask yourself, "What does the spirit wish?" The step of the spirit-knowledge is important. Approaching it, it seems that the spirit is most remote. But this is only apparently so; on the contrary, the spirit knocks powerfully. It is important to act directly, to grasp the spirit-knowledge. As one wishes, so should one act. One had better apply it on details than risk using it in massive measure.

121. Let us compare now the spirit-knowledge and the command of the will. The knowledge blossoms, manifesting protection and illumining the fundamentals. The command of the will is directed into alien spheres, and conquers and annexes. The command is denoted by the symbol of a sword and arrow. The symbol of the spirit-knowledge is a flower. The command can be communicated to the disciple from outside by a swift sending. Whereas, the spirit-knowledge blossoms from within, and cannot be evoked by any wand. Like a flower, the knowledge blooms in its destined hour.

How, then, may one assist the flower? Place it in a quiet spot, give it sunlight, and forbid anyone to touch and pluck the leaves. Without the spirit-knowledge one cannot raise to its height the knowledge predestined for humanity.

122. The growth of the works is similar to that of lilies. Near a garden wall one white sister has hidden herself. She has no companions, but the stalks already carry the evidence of new ones.

The incarnation as a flower is not often repeated. Some strive to the more massive forms of trees, but the charm of flowers is not always accessible, and one may not easily turn twice to them. There is no forbiddance against circumventing one of the animal incarnations by way of the plants. I would not say that the consciousness of many insects is superior to the consciousness of beautiful flowers. It is wise to outlive certain incarnations by sojourn as a flower. "Hasten, hasten! I will wait under a beautiful dome, and I will still be ahead of you." Thus, the path of beauty shortens the road.

123. To the deceiving one say, "How useful is thy deceit to me."

To the usurping one say, "Evidently the time has arrived for me to receive new things. But verily it is better for thee not to touch my things. Blasphemy and usurpation will attract lightning upon thee. Thy knife will be blunted by the invisible armor, and thou wilt destroy thy strongest weapons. And whither wilt thou go, consumed from within and reduced to ashes?"

I have told you of the smile and of strength. And to those sailing with Me a sword can be bestowed on the annual day of reminiscences. The law of requital triumphs, and those who gave shall receive.

Why do you follow Them? It is easy and useful to proceed with Them. Swift as the flight of the falcon; unexpected as the transformation of Jonah; inexhaustible as the flame! Only by renunciation, in spirit and upon Earth, do you attain the manifestation of light and truth. Inexhaustible is this Source!

On Earth, amidst threats, deprived of help and seemingly abased, they give, offer, endow, and follow the star. And, therefore, We rejoice on the anniversary night. And not only do they proceed to illumine the aura, but they go decisively, unrestrainedly. Therefore We rejoice!

124. Let us end the holiday and begin labor. Let us determine what to do. To act. In this eternal action is Our holiday. But you, following Our example, should act without distress. Resolve to act in calmness, bearing in mind that Our spring flows through you incessantly. And when you ask yourself—where are They Who made promises?—We are standing behind you; and We rejoice, measuring the growth of the flower of your aura. We rejoice because this is Our Garden. Beyond bounded vistas the Light unites the hearts.

125. Visions are as real as the phototelephone. One may consider them more real than the physical world. One may question only from which source they come; but the spirit controls this. To a good inquiry there will come a good answer.

I will say something of great importance: People study visions too little. It is precisely by following the character of the visions that the best history of the intellect may be written.

Even studying but the crude visions of the past, we discern definitely certain periods. Of course, visions of sensitive spirits have characteristic forms.

When men began to visualize Christ as an inaccessible idol, there began a period of visions of Christ in most realistic forms. He appeared as very close to men, entering into their daily life. Briefly speaking, every popular error is corrected. In the day of woman's humiliation one may trace the appearance of the Divine Mother.

Now, when the continuity of the chain between the earth and the heavens must be made evident, there is unity of manifestation upon various planes.

After St. Augustine the church began its plunge into the darkness of the Middle Ages, and Christ was locked behind a barrier of gold. In order to break it,

Christ Himself descended even in lesser Images in order to manifest again the grandeur of communion in unity. The wisdom of antiquity understood well the waves of the needs of the world.

Of course, one is the path from the One Source. As do the loftiest spirits, thus also the sensitive earthly apparati know this unity. The vortical gulf of rotation of the planets attracts particles of the spirit, and the World of Higher Reality flashes into the windows.

In the future equilibrium of spirit and matter a clear vision may be obtained. But now only fragments are to be seen. That is why the ancients guarded this natural telescope so cautiously. The most powerful telescopes were women, and the first requisite for their protection was quietude.

126. Here the Blessed One transmits; "All is for all and forever. Note the four laws: The Law of Containment; The Law of Fearlessness; The Law of Nearness; the Law of Righteousness."

It is not necessary to explain the Laws of Fearlessness and Righteousness, and it is easy to understand the Law of Containment, but the Law of Nearness must be elucidated. At the approach of certain Signs and Images ordained by dates, a specially saturated atmosphere gathers, as if clouds of smoke were overcasting Heaven and Earth. That which had been clear begins to crumble, and, as if in a whirlwind, falls to pieces. Even physically this period is difficult, but during this period certain dates are being pronounced which stand as milestones on the road.

However, knowing that the predestined people belong indefeasibly to the ordained dates, we must calmly pass through this period, like one becoming acclimated to new gases. Remember that during this period not only the Teacher but the whole Brotherhood is watching, and if individual voices are heard you need not be astonished. It is good to have flowers near during this period.

127. In the ancient magic books can be found the term, "Illuminacio Regale," which means the Royal Illumination. It is such an important principle that Hermes ends his treatise with the words, "Blessed are those who have chosen the path of Illumination."

The symbol of the anointing of kings has the same basis. Absolutely all initiates into the power of the Mysteries agree in the assertion that the highest harmony is in the manifestations of the power of Illumination. Therefore, the king is symbolically the anointed one, because without estranging himself from the earthly he expresses the will of Heaven. Above the conventional formulae that are congealed in the crust of prejudices there is knowledge, diffused, as it were, in the air.

Erect a lightning-rod and attract the heavenly arrow. For one it is dangerous, for another it is the best armor. And the whole future is based on attainment of Illumination. A most difficult telephone will be in the hands of man.

128. Not in jest are the planets beyond Uranus mentioned. Often the spirit struck by the cosmic whirl cannot acclimate itself and make observations, but this is only a question of time and technique. Our prolonged experiments will prepare for a great deal, as also for lengthy labor. Many of Our experiments require centuries. So if you feel the endlessness of labor, you know one more of Our feelings—all time is filled.

Sound and flowers become a necessity for further flights. The sounds of the life of the spheres and the vital emanations of flowers truly enter into the recipe of Amrita.

It is of great value to approach the highest ways without being a medium and without renouncing the earthly life. Where there is argument, where there is fear, where there is the germ of prejudice, there it is difficult for the white flowers. Simply, simply, simply, applying love, courage and readiness. This is no time for inflated bubbles; out of place is conceit, especially when compared with Christ's washing of the fishermen's feet.

In simplicity of life, in realization of the dignity of service to the New World, love for the worthy opens the Gates.

129. Just as We watch over you, so do We watch the development of children throughout the world from the cradle on, weighing their best thoughts. Of course, spirit does not often reach its best development, and the number of deserting ones is great, but We rejoice at a pure thought as at a beautiful garden. Therefore, do not be astonished that the Great Teacher repeats simple sentences, because by fixing these thoughts We sometimes provide opportunity for an excellent flower of spirit to become stronger.

Therefore, along with great cosmic discoveries and world events, We just as carefully cultivate the flowers of the spirit. Thus diversified is the labor of Our Brotherhood.

There is thought which leads inwardly, leaving the surface of the spirit unruffled, and there is also thought which flies into space as a projectile, carrying an explosive charge. A ray accompanies the flying bullet. Every spirit knows when thought flies like a boomerang. It is especially desirable that the thought be tinted by one's own color. But it is only opened nerve centers that do not give color to the thought, leaving it enwrapped in the color of the person; and then true individuality has begun. Instead of the thought's being colored by its contents, the whole sending is permeated by the color of the individuality. Thus is the ray physically formed.

The rainbow is the best sign; each allusion to a rainbow indicates the development of the third eye.

130. Christ said: "Not in a temple, but in spirit shalt thou pray." Verily, religious prejudice is the worst vulgarity. Often even religious ecstasies result in more harm than good. Out of them the crowd has made a vulgar spectacle. Therefore, it is important to show the vitality of Those Who stand upon all rungs of the Ladder.

It is time to cast off the diamonds which desecrate the holy Images. It is time to burn the relics, following the covenant of Christ. It is time to enter into the Temple of Spirit-understanding, consecrating one's forces which perfect the knowledge of the true power of spirit.

Not in remote laboratories, not in monastic cells, but in life shall you gather the truthful records. Where Christ, not in the folds of a chiton but in the beauty of toil, gathers the seekers of the freedom of the spirit.

Many times have saints returned to Earth because they had conveyed to the crowd too much of their exaltation instead of the structure of life.

We are absolutely averse to monasteries, as they are the antithesis of life. Only the seminars of life, communities of the best manifestation of labor, shall find Our assistance. Indeed, through life one must attain. It is precisely the generally-accepted religiousness that is unnecessary. The facts of conscious Communion with the Abode of Light are needed. Let us say we wish to bring help, so we proceed consciously without magic to the practical Source. In this simplicity is contained the entire current secret, as yet so inaccessible to men who walk up to their waists in prejudice. It is difficult for them to understand simplicity, beauty and fearlessness.

131. Fearlessness is Our leader. Beauty is Our ray of understanding. Simplicity is Our key to the secret doors of happiness.

You may write emphatically about simplicity, because nothing so much bars the way as the puffiness of self-conceit. One must exert utmost efforts to reject every germ of self-conceit, and without sinking into bigotry. It seems an old truth, but now it must be reiterated. Everyone must understand for himself where his simplicity is lacking.

132. Inasmuch as self-confidence is blessed in action, so is self-conceit ruinous. Self-conceit is hostile to simplicity. Even great minds are subject to this malady, and must return an additional time to labor until they eradicate this husk. One of the impeding conditions is lack of simplicity. One may wear bast-shoes and still not be simple. In simplicity one can build the greatest temple.

Simplicity, beauty and fearlessness—Christ and Buddha spoke of nothing more. And it is a blessing if the spirit vibrates to these covenants.

Do you notice that We even try to speak in the simplest words, only to bring nearer the downfall of the Tower of Babel? Hence, say that We shall reduce the dictionaries to ashes if they have made of the incisive words of Christ a heap of savage concepts. Simply it was said: "Pray in no wise but in the spirit."

Buddha passed through life in peace and people forgot him. Christ suffered and was forgotten. Now let each one raise his own glaive over his head, each according to his striving.

People, search amidst your rags! A white garment

is ready for all. Let us relegate all monkey attire to the circus, together with the conceited fools. Yes, yes, yes! It is better with savages than in a pharmacy of false remedies. Thus speak.

133. For the reason that Our pupils bear within themselves the microcosm of the Brotherhood, there is not an indifferent attitude towards them. In their mode of life the same details as of Our Life are gradually revealed. There is endless labor; absence of the sense of finiteness, even of knowledge; loneliness and the absence of a home on Earth; the understanding of joy, in the sense of realization of possibilities—for the best arrows so seldom reach their mark. And when We see the hearts of people who strive toward one and the same garden, how could We not manifest joy? But fearlessness in the face of endless labor is especially important. It is true that from the realization of the infinite possibilities of the human apparatus one feels relief.

The serpent of the solar plexus helps to surmount the confusion of the nerve centers; that is why the serpent was a regal symbol. When the coils of the serpent begin to curl, the organism becomes especially sensitive. Flowers transmit their vital emanation through the fibres of the tissues of the white blood corpuscles, which defend the citadel of the serpent. In nature, serpents love flowers; similarly, the serpent of the solar plexus is nourished by them.

Pigs also trample upon flowers, but without any effect on themselves. Therefore, without conscious consumption of the vital emanation one may pass over the best remedies. Hence the desire to see the flowers unplucked.

134. The refraction of rays yields sounds that enter into the symphony of the music of the spheres. One

may picture their crystalline quality of subtleness together with the power of the whirlwind.

There is a center in the brain which is called the bell. Like a resonator it gathers the symphony of the world, and it can transform the deepest silence into a thundering chord. It is said: "He who hath ears, let him hear."

The spinal chord is also called the spear, because if we wish to parry the blows we must tense this channel. The centers of the shoulders are also called wings, because during a self-sacrificing achievement rays extend from them. The legend concerning wings is highly symbolic. Likewise, it was a favorite custom of the ancients to wear a round metal plate upon their breasts.

The crown of the head is termed the well, because the waves of alien influences penetrate by this way. Everywhere in antiquity we see the covering of the head connected with the symbol of the priest, whereas now this symbol is replaced by the name of a business firm. So men have become spiritually bald!

Let us conclude with a message to the newcomers: There is so much for you to learn in order to acquire the wisdom of calmness and of actions. You must discern masked faces and know how to make My Name the armor of each action.

I will come unto the appointed country, and at that dawn one should not fall asleep. Therefore, learn to be sensitive and to keep about you a radiant garment. And when you are fatigued remember that inaction is unknown to Us. Try to adopt the same customs, and love flowers and sound.

Walk like lions, but guard the little ones, because they will help you to open My doors. Have understanding!

135. When many earthly apparati will have to be destroyed because of their harmfulness, it will then be time to bring humanity nearer by means of a natural apparatus.

An apparatus is a primary step. The true conquest will have been made when the spirit will have replaced all apparatus. For man to be fully equipped without a single machine—is it not a conquest!

The literate in letters can act only upon the surface of the Earth. The literate in spirit can operate beyond all boundaries.

The construction of New World combinations does not flow easily. The discarded centers attempt to obstruct the efforts of the new ones. We shall withstand the storm and downpour. Our mirror is bright.

136. Sensitive was your feeling that one should gather all courage to attain. There are tiresome and dangerous crossings, which may be endured only by trust in the Guide. He must lead you to the goal and not overstrain your strength. If He should overtax your forces, with what would He replace them?

The lofty mission of women must be performed by the woman. And in the Temple of the Mother of the World should abide the woman.

The manifestation of the Mother of the World will create the unity of women. The task now is to create a spiritually sovereign position for the woman. And the transmission to woman of direct communication with the Highest Forces is necessary as a psychological impetus. Of course, through the new religion will come the necessary respect.

I feel how strained the current is, how strained the atmosphere, but soon the pressure of the stars will be altered. Even the approach of the friendly planet brings difficulty, because its new rays are piercing the new strata of the atmosphere. Certainly, they are better than those of the moon, but the new pressure is not yet evenly distributed.

137. With profound symbolism, Christ pointed to the children. Just as simply let us approach the Gates of the Great Knowledge. True, We compose complicated and exact formulae, but the method of discovery lies in the spiritual consciousness. Precisely in this consciousness We find the means to add new spheres of the worlds accessible to thinking, extending the boundary of thinking. The consciousness thus merges into a bottomless ocean, as it were, embracing new spheres. Thus great and powerful is the creation of Cosmos.

138. Urusvati. It is time to say that this is the name we have given to the star which is irresistibly approaching the Earth. Since long ago it has been the symbol of the Mother of the World, and the Epoch of the Mother of the World must begin at the time of Her star's unprecedented approach to the Earth. The Great Epoch is beginning, because the spirit understanding is linked with the Mother of the World. Even to those who know the date it is marvelous to behold the physical approach of the predestined. The approach of this very great Epoch is important; it will substantially change the life of the Earth. A Great Epoch! I rejoice so much, seeing how the new rays are piercing the thickness of the Earth. Even though in the beginning they are hard to bear, yet their emanation induces new elements, so needed for the impetus. New rays are reaching the Earth for the first time since its formation.

Today is the beginning of the feminine awakening. A new wave has reached Earth today, and new hearths have become alight; for the substance of the rays penetrates deeply.

It is joyous to feel the approach of the New Epoch.

139. The necessity of deceit compels the priests of the old religions to push the people into the abyss of darkness. Yes, one may leave them at the foot of the mountain, as did Moses, but the tablets of the Commandments must be manifested.

How perishable everything once seemed! Our disciples, appearing for the last time on Earth, experience the feeling of loneliness and of estrangement. Only in consciousness do we understand the value of Earth, but nothing compels us to look back if the spirit has already filled its treasure chest. The chief requisite is the modification of the human feeling of joy. And what joy may there be, when one realizes the imperfection of life? But when the spirit faces the dimensions of Cosmos, then this joy is replaced by the realization of possibilities.

And when I whispered, "Thy joy will depart," I had in mind the transformation of human joy into the cosmically manifested conception as if by entering into a vacuum. The rays of the new life enwrap one better than mosquito netting, and one need not strain oneself toward the Earth. In this, when we are working for the Earth, there is harmony. For outsiders, this seems sheer nonsense, but you understand how one can grasp and develop each pure earthly thought beyond its contemporary import. And when one has traced the thread from Christ to the blade of grass, then only has the scope of work been covered.

Great is the knowledge of the absence of death. All has been forgotten—otherwise men would live differently.

140. This is the story of Mary Magdalene:

You know my way of life, how by night people knew us and by day shunned us. So with Christ. By night they came and by day they averted their faces. I thought: "Here am I, the lowest, and by sunlight people are ashamed of me. But He also, the most Exalted Prophet, is avoided by day. Thus, the lowest and the loftiest are equally avoided."

And so I decided to find Him by day, and to stretch out my hand to Him. I donned my best attire and my necklace from Smyrna, and perfumed my hair. And so I went, to say to people: "Here by daylight are met the lowest and the highest—equally avoided by you."

And when I saw Him, seated among the fishermen and covered with a sackcloth, I remained on the opposite side and could not approach. Between us people passed, equally avoiding us. Thus my life was determined. Because He said to His most beloved disciple: "Take this pinch of dust and bring it to this woman, that she may exchange it for her necklace. Verily in these ashes is more life than in her stones; because from ashes I may create stones but from stones only dust."

The rest you already know. He did not condemn me. He but weighed my chains and the chains of shame crumbled as dust. He decided simply. Never did He hesitate to send the simplest object which determined one's entire life. He touched these sendings as though bathing them in spirit. His path was empty; because people, after receiving His gifts, hastily departed. And wishing to lay on His Hands, He found all empty. When He was already condemned, the furies of shame rushed behind Him and mockingly brandished their branches. The price of the robber was worthy of the crowd.

Verily He cleft asunder the chains because He bestowed knowledge without accepting reward.

141. With what diversity do the plans of constructions proceed!

Time was when We said: "Give up everything." Now We go further and say: "Take everything but do not consider it your own."

Simple reasoning will show how impossible it is to take earthly things along with one. But they have been created with the participation of the spirit; hence, one should not despise them. How can one pass by the flowers of nature? But the creations of labor are also the flowers of humanity. If their scent and color are imperfect, one can but regret it.

142. Thus, each useful thought finds approval. A stroke upon the string calls forth a consonance. A clear and courageous formulation of thought is very useful.

We can appreciate a mediaeval lute as well as Wagner's "Walküre." Also fine is the ancient Chinese crystal instrument. The purity of its tone corresponds to the purity of flowers. It is called a rainbow harp. The rays produce excellent trumpet sounds, and the vortex rings are irreplaceable, as in a string ensemble. Verily, it is worth-while living with such perspectives.

143. In conformity with the rhythm of World Motion, repetitive accrual of power is needed. The display of haste is adverse to the World's creation

The way of formation of crystals and flowers indicates how perfection develops.

144. The link between Christ and Buddha glows dimly in people's understanding.

145. Regarding the application of My medicines, all the powers of the vegetable kingdom must be directed toward the one aim for which they exist—the increase of vitality. It is possible to cure all ailments by the counterpoising of vitality.

Certain plants exist as reservoirs of prana. The pine trees collect it as if in electric needles. And as a bond between heaven and the depths of earth, the earth is covered with living antennae which gather and preserve the true renewing element of the spiritual tissue.

Ignorance may conceal a malady, but it is better to consume it with the fire of life. Not by an artificial, depleting stimulant, but by using the life force to restore the balance.

One should not search among the minerals, because they have long ago become devoid of the effect of prana. Their destination is different. But the solar manifestation bestows life.

Truly, the mineral soil provides a seeming foothold on life; but this is only a pedal, which is useless without strings. And so, My pharmacy will be directed toward the essence which is common to mankind. It will affirm vitality without any slaughter, because the plants pass easily into the next state.

Inoculations are good if the vitality is equal to them, otherwise they are like a destructive plaster. A being who possesses full vitality is in no need of inoculations; he has the so-called solar immunity.

There is little vitality in the villages, because prana helps only when absorbed consciously. Nourishment of the spirit can proceed only consciously.

To the indications about medicines one should add that the skins of the musk animals were valued in Lemuria. Also, a chalice of cedar resin figured in the rituals of the consecration of the kings of the ancient Khorassan. Druids also called the chalice of cedar resin the chalice of life. And only later, with the loss of the realization of the spirit, was it replaced by blood.

The fire of Zoroaster was the result of burning of the cedar resin in the chalice.

146. Half of the sky is occupied with an unusual manifestation. Around an invisible luminary an immeasurable circle has begun to radiate, rays rushing

along its brim. The furies of terror have concealed themselves within caves, suffocated by the radiance of this sign.

The best abilities have been borne by the people. The giving hand lives wisely. And let the old lands rest. To whom to give the new soil? To those who will bring a pinch of the old Knowledge. The knot of peoples is fastened upon an empty place. Let the departed ones return.

Since seas can cover the mountains, and deserts can replace the sea-bottoms, then is it impossible to visualize the miracle of populating the desert? A ploughman, a simple husbandman, gives rest to his field, permitting it to become covered with weeds. Likewise, in the Great Plan the places of harvest must be alternated. It is befitting for the new to be upon a new place.

I feel the human spirit will rise; but welcome the most unfortunate ones: "Come, ye naked, we will clothe thee; come, ye little ones, we will rear thee; come, ye dumb ones, we will give thee speech; come, ye blind ones, and see the predestined domain."

Whose hand is stretching forth to the bolt of My House? Travelers, thou art without belongings; therefore thou shalt enter.

Thus will we attain.

147. It is time to do away with the imperfection of matter. For this the people must become conscious of the spirit; otherwise the general condition tends to reduce the individual possibilities to its own level, as the waves of the ocean preserve a common rhythm.

Therefore, it is time to arouse the nations by sword or lightning, only to evoke the cry of the spirit.

148. Could you but see the cliches of the first creations, you would be horrified. The chief obstacle is that matter can be acted upon only by matter. To construct

a bridge from the spirit to the Brotherhood was not so difficult, but to establish a normal link between the Brotherhood and the people is unspeakably difficult. Men, like parrots, repeat the remarkable formula, "Death conquers death"—but they do not consider its meaning.

It has been decided to safeguard the future destiny by placing it into vital practical conditions of the cooperation of the spirit. The difficulty lies in the new differentiations of humanity. The former primitive divisions into castes, classes and professions have been replaced by a complicated distinction according to light and shade. This manifestation, as a purified communism, will select the best groups of humanity. Without details, one must trace a general demarcation line of light and shade, as if recruiting a new army.

How difficult it is to select without having recourse to special measures!

149. The waves of the currents proceed spirally. The principle of the spiral whirl is found in everything.

150. The Mother of the World appears as a symbol of the feminine Origin in the new epoch, and the masculine Origin voluntarily returns the treasure of the World to the feminine Origin. Amazons were the embodiment of the strength of the feminine Principle, and now it is necessary to show the aspect of spiritual perfection of woman.

In the name of Christ great crimes have been committed. Therefore, Christ nowadays clothes Himself in other garments. One must discard all the exaggerations. We are not speaking of slightly embellished works only, as even through the volumes of Origen corrections were slipped in. Therefore, it is time to change conditions in the world.

The springs cannot act before the appointed date, and to hasten means to cut the wires.

151. We cannot know the limits of possibilities of conquests of the spirit. The seed of the spirit is self-containing, but according to the aura its striving can be judged.

There are thoughts directed inwardly and absorbed by the potentiality of the spirit. There are thoughts which are not manifested upon the earthly plane.

152. One may build a city, one may give the best knowledge, but most difficult of all is to reveal the true Image of Christ. Think, how to cleanse the Image of Christ.

Gathering the crumbs of the people's concept of the Savior and replacing the chiton by overalls, one can find illumination.

By human hands must the Temple be built.

153. The Star of Allahabad pointed out the way. And so We visited Sarnath and Gaya. Everywhere We found the desecration of religion. On the way back, under the full moon, occurred the memorable saying of Christ.

During the night march the guide lost his way. After some seeking I found Christ seated upon a sand mound looking at the sands flooded by moonlight. I said to Him, "We have lost the way. We must await the indication of the stars."

"Rossul Moria, what is a way to Us, when the whole world is awaiting Us?"

Then, taking His bamboo staff, He traced a square around the impression of His foot, saying "Verily, by human feet."

And making the impression of His palm, He surrounded it also with a square. "Verily, by human hands."

Between the squares He drew the semblance of a pillar surmounted by an arc. He said: "O how Aum shall penetrate into the human consciousness! Here I have drawn a pistil and above it an arc, and have set the foundation in four directions. When by human feet and human hands the Temple will be built wherein will blossom the pistil laid by Me, then let the Builders pass by My Way. Why should We await the way, when it is before Us?"

Then, rising, He effaced with His cane all that He had drawn.

"When the Name of the Temple will be pronounced, then shall the inscription emerge. In remembrance of My constellation, the square and nine stars shall glow over the Temple. The sign of the foot and the hand shall be inscribed above the Cornerstone."

Thus He Himself spoke of the eve of the new moon.

And the heat of the desert was great.

The Star of the Morning is the sign of the Great Epoch which will flash as the first ray from the Teaching of Christ. For who is to extol the Mother of the World if not Christ, the One so demeaned by the world.

Give Us the Arch of the Dome, wherein to enter.

154. The touch of the ray of the Brotherhood increases the sagacity of perceptions. Therefore, one must take into consideration every sensation.

Small as well as important events strike upon the aura, as upon musical strings. The growing aura has its advantages, and these Aeolian wings multifariously resound. The burden of the world plays its symphonies upon them. One cannot say that a man illumined by the aura is motionless. The outer shell of the aura is like a surging sea. What a talk for the scientist—to trace the nourishment of the aura from within and the reflection from without! Verily a world battle!

The symbol of the burden of the world is a man carrying a sphere. All complex sensations are increased to the point of pain. An impression can be received as of being between the hammer and anvil. Therefore, the attainment of a rainbow aura is so practical, because it carries within itself the means of assimilation of all that exists. Even the best monochromatic auras must quench the conflagrations by themselves, drawing from their own ocean. Whereas a rainbow aura easily repels and takes in the rays. Therefore, achievement is a most practical action.

155. When in perplexity, sit together in silence and think one thought. Soon you will understand to what an extent such silent counsel is practical. We precipitate the force of the spirit along one channel. An unusual discharge results, reinforced by magnetism and harmonized by rhythm. The law is that two concordant thoughts increase the power seven times. This is not magic but a practical consideration.

156. Know how to meet the waves of life in beauty. It is not the receiving of sweet pastry but the forging of a sword; not sugared fingers but the strong hand of a warrior of spirit. To encounter the enemy without acknowledging him as such, and to reach the Gates without looking back—is Our way! We know the gait of the destined conquerors. Chiefly, do not jump along the way. The main thing is that We should rejoice at the steadiness of your pace. It is more fitting for the ray to illumine the walking ones than to leap after the jumping ones. People have been able to do much, but seldom did they know how to end in beauty. At dawn, at eventide, in advance and retreat, flying or diving, think about Us, the Watching Ones. The beautiful will be also the worthy. Must one open the pages of history to show giants at a loss how to step over a stream? Easiness was then obscured by unsightliness, and the mind faltered, losing appreciation of beauty. But the

manifestation of complicated problems means to the mathematician only joy. And there remains the power of silence, which has already been spoken about.

157. Fire singes imperfect thoughts. How else to fill the cradle of authentic achievements? The experiment of filtering the thought through the ray is very important. Everyone expresses the essence of his aura, but single thoughts can be of different value according to their spiritual consistency. Then the substance of the thought can be tested by a special ray. The presence of inner spirituality illumines the thought by the color of the aura, but if the thought is a base one it burns under the ray. Thus, there results not only a testing of thought but also a disinfection of space.

One may imagine how a ray penetrates the space and finds wonderful treasures as well as little red and orange fires, which are like criminal poisoners. Why then not purify the layers above Earth, when even to the eye they are of a smoky orange color?

The best thing is to destroy the germs of base thoughts, which are more infectious than all diseases. One should be careful not so much about uttered words as about thoughts. During one word ten thoughts are born.

158. It is necessary to speak truthfully about the fundamentals. You noticed that We call the astral world a heaped-up pile. We emphasize how We avoid it. You know already that astral bodies have volume and weight and carry away with them many peculiarities of earthly life. The relativity of earthly knowledge is well-known. Of course, the astral bodies carry away with them not a small share of relativeness, but, being freed from the carnate shell, they acquire creativeness of the spirit. But you can picture to yourselves how the relativity of knowledge is reflected in these structures.

Alongside an imagined Olympus, one may encounter a monstrous factory, unrealized during the earthly life. There exist harmonious oases, but in general there prevails a fantastic cemetery of human survivals. It is inadvisable to delve far into the astral cliches, because only an erroneous presentation will follow. In this the usual mediums are harmful.

Let us not enumerate the consequences of the fumes of the earthly kitchen, but it is quite important to understand how one may mitigate the consequences of relativity. They may be mitigated by the actual truth; but the truth may be realized only through spirituality, and therefore the awakening of spirituality becomes a cosmic condition.

159. Joy is a special wisdom, as Christ said.

Nothing gathers the essence of prana as well as do plants. Even pranayama may be replaced by association with plants. And it should be understood how assiduously the eye must fathom the structure of the plants. The pores of the plants are enlarged not only by the advent of new leaves and flowers, but also by the removal of dead parts. The law of Earth's nurture affords, through the antennae of the plants, the possibility of drawing out of this reservoir by means of smell and sight the precious quality of vitality, the so-called Naturovaloris, which is acquired through conscious striving.

Valuable as are the living plants which have not lost their vitality, preparations from them dried in the sun may also be useful. But the stage of decomposition should be avoided, because decomposition is the same in everything and always attracts the most imperfect spirits. Therefore, one should watch the condition of cut flowers. The smell of decomposition must be sensed, as it is not the external appearance but the smell which manifests the symptom.

When it is not the season for flowers, it is useful to have small pine trees. Like a dynamo they accumulate vitality, and they are more effectual than right breathing. Instead of by ritual breathings one can thus receive a most condensed supply of prana. Of course, a state of rest also increases the action.

Vital understanding of the power of nature will provide without magic a renovation of possibilities.

160. It is impossible to separate the conditions of Earth from surrounding conditions, because the mental world has no narrow boundaries.

Again one must speak against the astral world, because it is desirable in the future to shorten considerably this stage. Now it is unavoidable, but upon development of the spirit the manifestation of the mental body becomes more attainable.

Devachan is the place of pleasant realizations. But at the same time it is dangerous, because a weak spirit is reluctant to leave so pleasant a station. This station yields the greatest unwillingness to return for more labor. And when the time comes to leave this Valhalla, while the mental body impels one to achievement, the astral body finds the place most comfortable.

It is precisely the spirit which does not permit stopping, for the spirit in its innermost self remembers beautiful worlds. Beyond all the recollections abides an inexpressible, firm consciousness of the possibility of return to the Light whence the spark emanated.

How can a sensitive spirit avoid the onset of world anguish? There has never been a case of a man being able to detach himself in spirit from the earthly plane without contraction of his nerve centers, exactly like that of the daring aviator who feels

66

a singular tremor in his heart upon detaching himself from the Earth.

The goal and the meaning of existence is to strive upward beyond the limits of the known, and to help one another.

If, without any mechanics, we recall the sensation of standing on a rock before a phenomenon of nature, does not the heart contract from rapture? After this stage, the sensation of embracing boundlessness will be realized.

Some people are easily reconciled to the sham and luxury of the astral plane, but you will not be attracted by it. Only the abodes of knowledge will outline the path.

161. You have noticed that each Great Teacher has spoken about the continuity of life. One may also notice that it is just this indication which is expurgated from each teaching, because materialism must defend itself. On Earth this condition is of special importance.

It must be known that the earthly matter is very dense. On the planets of lower level than Earth the matter is very coarse; upon those higher than Earth, matter harmonizes with the spirit. Hence, the Earth appears as a turning point.

There are imperfections upon higher planets, but there is not the resistance of matter. It is easier to search there without loosing one's strength in needless struggle. There matter becomes inseparable from spirit, without any opposition between them.

No one denies the value of matter, but it is inconceivable that on a locomotive the wheels and the boiler must quarrel. It seems that the better the boiler works the better it is for the wheels. But the one in charge of the wheels might think that they are the most important part of the organism and invite everyone to take a ride on the wheels, ignoring the fact that without the steam power the wheels can only roll downhill.

Fundamentally, the structure of matter and spirit contains no conflict. Why arrest the motion into the beautiful Infinite? And why pile up illusory dams near the Earth?

One may pity the retarded travelers, because these earthly stations will not serve them beyond a certain period.

Why are a hundred incarnations necessary, when with ten one may cross the threshold?

How vivid the recollection that the last Great Teacher suffered an outrageous death for what would seem to have been already long since known to humanity!

162. One should have in mind that refined matter has an absorptive quality. When someone approaches matter for the sake of its immediate condition, he does not receive immunity of the spirit and sinks into the so-called maya, because without the perfecting of the substance of things their shell becomes poisonous.

163. The growth of spiritual understanding attracts also the cooperation of the small entities which populate the air. This is why the hostility of matter is to be regretted. Conscious cooperation with matter could be reached far sooner.

It is tempting to receive immediate material advantages. Even intelligent men have no objection to receiving a title, not weighing its consequences. The cemetery is full of high titles; this is the memorial to that fence which is the insulation of matter.

Indeed matter is very important, but only with spirit does it attain its sacred significance. As the great admirer of matter without spirit is illiterate, so lacking would be an adept without intellect. Yet one can fly in spirit, while matter has no wings. Spirituality on Earth can open towering Gates.

When man is free from fear, he can know the origin of reality.

164. The quality of rays is infinitely varied, but two categories of rays are easy to distinguish. One category can be revealed to contemporary humanity, while the other comprises rays demanding from people a spiritual understanding without which the rays may be very destructive. Each ray can manifest a defense only within the limits of its generic colors. If even a very deep yellow is discordant for a violet ray, then how will all the crimson-toned ones strike the outer shell of such aura? Through perfection a new defense is attained, whereupon we cognize various rays, absorbing them with our own ray. We shield ourselves, as it were, against fatigue from various flashes by our own gamut of colors.

For instance, someone possessing a violet aura begins to see everything in waves of violet and blue tints. This means that his shield is becoming stronger.

It means that instead of receiving stings and wounds, he is immersed in his own ocean, and alien colors are seemingly absorbed by the accumulations of his aura. But the difficulty of these accumulations is that they cannot be superimposed from without and can be only evoked from within. Therefore, it is a good sign when the flame of the spirit radiates its own color.

Each monochromatic aura contains within itself three waves, corresponding to the three chief substances: physical, astral and mental.

165. We see the march of predestined events and note the appearance of quiet figures who are seemingly detached from life, although We value them by their achievements. But their lives flow on amidst now

a kind of detachment and now an achievement, which appears like a spark in the darkness.

The subsequent as well as the early events pass utterly unnoticed. The throne, or the cell of a monastery, or the cobbler's nook have no importance; the previously accumulated aura accompanies this last path. Of course the aura expands, and, as it were, shields an unusual sensitiveness; but its quality no longer changes, and from early age one may distinguish these singular children, who carry their own world of manifestations of the spirit.

Very rarely, almost never, do they limit themselves to a single specialty. Actually, the absence of specialty is characteristic; hands seem to be stretched out to the chalice.

Looking into past lives, one may see representatives of religion, kingdoms, science, art and mechanics, waiting and prepared for the journey and ready to depart at any hour without regrets.

The combination of a correct appreciation of the beauty of matter with a readiness to fathom the attainments of the spirit, brings the achievement to maturity. The turmoil of life no longer attracts, and of course there comes the realization that it can proceed no further in the same way.

The achievement may be either comparatively transient or instantaneous. The realization of the necessity to express a definite action is brought from afar, and it is accomplished as simply as any daily deed.

And so, the most difficult thing is to encompass both the rapture of matter and the manifestations of spirit. And how many wondrous quests have been delayed by a regret concerning matter, or by spiritual insulation. Sometimes the affinity of the spirit with matter is easily achieved; then one should look for the cause in the past chosen lives.

The most extreme ascetic, who curses the beauty of the world, closes the Gates before himself. Likewise, the scientist who forgets about the Source deprives himself of flights into the domain of higher conquests. Children will grasp this simple condition, but many adults reject it as nonsense.

Only by special ways of communication can those in the train of achievement move on. And to await the timeliness of that which the spirit considers and knows becomes so painful that it is as if the time had stopped, and some sort of conflagration had destroyed the accumulated wealth.

Truly did Christ say: "You know neither the day nor the hour." He also revealed another truth in saying, "Why hast Thou forsaken me, O Lord?" This refers to the knowledge of the spirit. At the last moment, before the consummation of the earthly cycle, we sink into a seeming vacuum, in order that all the accumulated fires may flash out at once. By restraining the consciousness of the past the leap over the abyss is achieved.

166. Even earthly things may have a special atmosphere preserved around them. Just before reading a document one may become impressed by a sense of the nature of it. The Teaching penetrates considerably further when first of all it is possible to transmit the essence of a manifestation. I vouch that very soon sensitive apparati will be able to assimilate it. The intuition unfolds normally if spirit is acknowledged.

Especially often do people say, "We are no longer astonished at anything," and forthwith they are astonished at the first inexplicable creak.

Now you will ask why the solitude of the last incarnation is necessary. This is a circumstance very difficult to explain from the earthly point of view, but simple and immutable as soon as one crosses beyond the line of earthly existence. Even in the ordinary approach of a ship to a harbor one observes a similar manifestation. The life of the ship ceases; the journey is ending and the passengers are busy with the matter of disembarking, and the recent united activities seem non-existent.

How much more so is the feeling of an organism approaching a condition of complete change. The flow of striving toward the means of expression of the last action is guided by intuition.

167. It also happens that before departure all voices become silent, and, even being aware of this law, one becomes awed.

In the Egyptian Mysteries there was a fixed moment when the neophyte, having been placed before a threshold in absolute darkness, had to enter into the Unknown without slackening his steps.

Especially nowadays, since Christ has renounced the miracles, this moment into the Unknown must be passed by special means. Because the future epoch must erase the boundaries between the worlds. And the Egyptian Mysteries have been transformed into the formula, "by human feet."

168. A protective net must surround the body. It is very important that the aura terminate in a net of vital sparks; therefore, even purple and blue auras must have ruby-colored sparks at their periphery. The display of those tones which are foreign to

Earth makes the possessor too sensitive to earthly manifestations. The width of the aura often grows, the insignia of Earth being thrust out. Teros and Tamas must work like brothers, because the representatives of Tamas and Teros must be inseparable.

The spirit imbues the aura with radiation, but the

network makes it compact. By the realization of the defensive net one can protect the radiations; but it is impossible to stretch the network without Teros, the ray of which, like a lantern, must find the break. Hence, there can follow the non-coordination of contact with the outer world. This simple condition must be especially assimilated, because the network is regulated by the usual consciousness and the command of the will.

At first glance the leaping sparks seem to be only the motion of an apparatus; but they are guardians, ready to repel the enemy.

169. It may now be told why it was decided to renounce the miracles. The way of miracles is most remote from harmony. Either the miracle is lost, and then it is simply harmful; or it jerks a man up to a degree which cannot be maintained under surrounding conditions; or it happens to be seen by envious ones, whereupon it begets evil.

Courageously to know the possibility of penetrating the full light, and consciously to conceal the unusual manifestations, means to bring harmony nearer. Proceeding by way of the broadening of consciousness is the approach to true action.

The ray of understanding of the predestined immensity of the manifestations of power can unite ready souls, and without this readiness any miracle is turned into a curiosity.

One may have at one's disposal powers not for demonstration but for progressive actions. When the essence is invisible to the crowd and arouses no attention, being veiled by the result, such essence will penetrate into the consciousness of the people, accustoming them to the fact of achievement through human hands. Thus, actions will be achieved by human hands as a result of the highest spirit-creativeness.

It behooves the spirit to dwell in spirit. Let the hand manifest the earthly direction; creation by human hands does not arouse hatred.

In antiquity, when communicating the commandments of God it was customary to cover the face. Later, people tried to overcome matter by proclamation of powers they had not yet mastered. Of course, this gave birth to the Inquisition. The essence of the Inquisition was persecution of the unusual.

To make of the unusual the predestined, as a result of cooperation, will be to compel its acceptance by even the most dull ones. Therefore, let the miracles remain only in the consciousness of a few who are able to look into the Infinite!

Thus, there is obtained a reversal of the procedure of antiquity. Formerly the priests guarded the miracles for the crowds; now the miracles are for the priests.

The striving towards a true cooperation lies at the foundation of evolution. Only by the awakening of creativeness may the march of ignorance be destroyed. Though its forms be even monstrous, though the sun be made in a back yard out of chips, still the foaming torrent will break through the walls of matter. New discoveries will stimulate the collecting. Instead of stock market speculation let there be striving for discoveries, supported by cooperative societies.

170. The chaos of the chips can be understood through beauty. What other measure can be applied to the medley of thought dross? And when you find a heap of goodness, readiness and movability, you can set to work only with the shovel of beauty. A wonderful fire is contained in the communion with people.

Discontent is only the knowledge of possibilities. Contentment is the death of the spirit.

171. Where the people are expectant, We send thither Our chosen ones.

Above the earthly rays blaze the rays of spirit. Burn the garments of the past day. The mole is not a fit companion. I affirm that at the destined hour all the moles in the world will not be able to dig a ditch. Hands off, hands off, hands off!

Our Shield is forged by human hands. The manifested power will come through people. There is no need for angels to deafen the ears with trumpets when human hands are found able to accept the chalice.

172. The standardized life must be skillfully avoided. The best people are in advance of the world, which is burdened by clouds.

He who wishes to reach the New Country must not only cast aside all prejudices but also enter by a new way.

The affirmation of life must be built upon the application to local conditions. Where there are a hundred languages spoken, one must understand a hundred psychologies. One expression for all is like a stereotyped column of a state building.

Unity in variety gives the best harvest result. The fruit must be grown by the grafting of new, necessary currents. Therefore, We shall often speak about the New Country—this is most urgent.

173. From small to great, from a daily matter up to worlds, do we wander; but no one will call this insignificant, and never will the result prove to be incorrect.

One will ask why the Teaching is strewn like seeds.

Answer that only out of a variety of threads can one create a complex pattern.

One will ask why the Teaching has no completed tenets. Answer that because in completeness there is death.

One will ask why the parts of the Teaching cannot be connected logically. Answer that it would be ugly to grow only a head or only a hand.

One will ask why there is not pronounced first the formula of Heaven and later the conjuration of the Earth. Answer that each thread of the garment of the Mother runs throughout, from the top to the bottom, and vice versa.

One will ask why the predestined cannot be manifested at once. Answer that the pillars of a house are erected in successive order. And if the workmen say, "Let us set them all at once," the builder answers, "Do you wish to destroy them!" Thus, a drop contains the whole world.

The manifestation of unlimited possibilities will give you calmness for perception.

How then does an earthquake reverberate upon all that exists? Also various winds and storms? How are the diverse auras of people reflected upon plants? An entirely new institute for research could be established.

Truly, the thread of cosmic coordination can be found by comparing the pulse of different elements.

There is nothing new in this; but the importance of world-wide cooperation can be demonstrated graphically, even to some readers whose spirits are like cockroaches sticking in corners.

Sow more broadly than the broad. Announce in schools a prize for the greatest quantity of submitted questions. Heretofore one has been rewarded for answers, now it should be for questions.

174. Before the astral body sets out there is an outflow from the vertebrae. The various nerve centers unfold differently, and the time comes when this difference must be normalized by rest, just as a tuned

piano should not be touched for awhile nor pounded with any metallic object.

An entire rock can be split when knocked upon by metal in a discordant tone. Although this manifestation is well known, it is difficult to imagine it in connection with the human organism. Only by experience can one sense how much more shocking than an explosion some whispers are. It must also be remembered that the combinations of nerves are so diverse that it is difficult to determine the effects by any laws.

The physical condition and the spirit are so closely interrelated that only by personal experience can one determine how to safeguard the correct approach of the fires. Fires are the wells of the rays.

175. World thought transmits world decision, and the construction of the New Country can only be in world-wide understanding.

Do We need eloquence? The way of the contact of the spirit is much more powerful. When you see how with one gesture great decisions are executed, it becomes clear how valuable words are; not in quantity nor in their outer form but in their inner essence.

One must speak still more concisely. The blacksmith must not use the hammer jarringly. The Teaching of Christ can be inscribed upon the palm of the hand.

176. The flight of the spirit is not reckoned in hours. The manifestation of the spirit rushing between the planets is beyond time; a moment, because it cannot be extended. Otherwise there results a rupture between the densified body and the mental. But one should remember that the spirit, which acts beyond time, also cognizes beyond the limitation of numbers, and is able to cognize up to the fourteenth gradation of hearing, whereas on the earthly sphere one can attain only up to the ninth.

The gradations of hearing permit one to make various elements the coworkers of man. The sound of the rain is also not without significance. Many ways will enrich the earthly creativeness.

177. Gloom can be dispersed by changing the direction of thoughts. Not words, but the runners of thought weave the aura. We are desirous of making Our works profitable in both the spiritual and material sense. I affirm that for this the quality of thoughts has great importance.

One must stress benevolent and useful unity, and that We appraise foolishness at its worth. Of course, in a great work foolishness may also find a lodging, but not on the top floor.

Everyone can exist, but the future world requires the enlightenment of consciousness and not the muttering of lofty expressions.

We appreciate a business-like financial account more than a string of pompous phrases. One must think about the world and manifest practical thoughts.

On the eve of advent of the New Temple one must manifest resourcefulness and show the people an extraordinary alertness of mind. To walk in swaddles is not comfortable.

178. I attest that it is easier to cross the mountains than to straighten out a human tail. Our Ray is directed in full search. One must understand Our Shield—verily, courage is needed.

179. In a rational religion there is no perplexity.

180. They who deny God have not seen Him. But what does the God of the tavern-keepers look like? And great would be the corruption of a Christ who would cover any treason for a candle!

There is nothing worse than a candle of villany. Christ does not need such worshippers, for the smoke of their candles is smutting His garment. The waters of Jordan and Urdar could not cleanse away the traces of such offerings.

181. A legend about Buddha.

A righteous man wished to see Buddha. His attention being kept upon a wide variety of objects, his hands did not grasp images of wisdom, his eyes did not penetrate objects of reverence, and the manifestation did not come.

Finally, bending low in prayer, the seeker felt a thread of a web descend on his forehead. He cast it away. Then a clear voice rang out, "Why dost thou reject My Hand? My Ray has followed thee. Permit me to embrace thee."

Then the sun serpent became atremble in the man and he sought the rejected thread. And in his hands it turned into forty pearls. And each bore the Image of Buddha. In their center was a stone, and upon it the inscription: "Valor—despair—joy."

The follower of Buddha received joy because he knew the path to it.

I am thinking of wings. The works are verily winged. The steeds are speeding through the earthly spaces, and as whirlwinds the creative strivings are borne along. Onward to battle! battle! battle!

Verily, the majestic is the picture of the ocean of the spirit! The sound of the call drones and rings out, and they who have accepted the weapon of the spirit are striving toward the Altar, because the daughter of the world has completed her spiritual raiment.

Onward to battle! battle! battle!

"I hear the call and bow my head before the Command of the Blessed Lord."

182. One must speak about those who oppose and threaten Me. It is light-minded to hope that a rent in

the web of the world can be easily mended. Even a simple sound may bring an unexpected echo from afar. How much deeper does the sending of the spirit pierce into space! And these wounds are almost unhealable.

The hand which has inflicted a wound upon the Design of the Lords rejects the Shield. One can demolish a house, one can cut a tree asunder, but how can one impede the plan of the Lords?

I pronounce not a threat but a simple deduction. If a man has approached the cosmic whirl, then any deviation brings on the next wave, and to fall under it is as to fall under the heel of a giant.

We ask in kindness not to reject the Guiding Hand. Woe to the one remaining behind!

And what honor is it to inflict a wound on Me?

First return all thou has received from Me. But thou canst not do it, even if thou wouldst add the liver and the heart.

Wouldst thou strike Him Who gave thy talent to thee? Wherein, then, wouldst thou differ from a plunderer? Do not besmirch the Hand of the Giving One, else this dirt turn into thy leprosy.

That is why Our Brotherhood esteems the conception of gratitude. Therefore, understand thy benefit.

183. The Teaching about sacrifice was already given to you. Sacrifice is power. Power is possibility. Consequently every sacrifice is first of all a possibility.

It is time to cast aside the hypocrisy that sacrifice is deprivation. We do not accept deprivations, but We give possibilities.

Let us see what possibilities are born from the so-called sacrifice. Where is a true sacrifice which can demean? In Our Treasury there is a large collection of sacrifices, and each one was useful to the one who made it. We dislike to speak about sacrifices, because a sacrifice is the most profitable undertaking.

Small tradesmen love to cry about the expenditures and to feign a loss. But a real provider in life considers each expenditure as only a business guarantee. You have lost not through sacrifice but pillage.

Christ advised to distribute spiritual wealth. But, as the keys to it are far away, people have applied this advice toward the distribution of pillaged money. First to steal and then to give away with a tear and become enraptured by one's own goodness. As if in speaking of distribution the Teacher could have had in mind chairs and old coats! The Teacher meant imponderable wealth. Only the spiritual gift can move the cup of the scales.

Let us examine the row of coworkers. Was anyone deprived of anything? No, all have been enriched. Is it not enrichment to become a ruler of a new kingdom? So rich is that kingdom that without too much harm we can break a few dishes. Positively the hands are growing, and the book of gratitude can be examined.

I advise the providers in life to have substitutes for all positions.

In large enterprises the business stands upon the business, and not upon personality.

Who can justly assert that he has been the giving one? We will open Our account books and show how much every one received. For it is not at all easy to sacrifice when a sacrifice is a possibility, and the possibility is a benefit, and the benefit is a sound cooperation, and a cooperation is the Alatir-Stone, which either resurrects or consumes.

But self-abnegation can open the Gates of Understanding, and the decrepit sacrifice of unneeded things will swing upon one branch with self-love.

184. Every incarnation carries a connection with a certain character of one's past lives which is most closely in keeping with the era. The knowledge of previous manifestations can help the vigilant in spirit, but it is harmful to the slumbering ones. The lunar life must be outlived.

185. Regarding the infallibility and movability of the plan, these conditions are especially difficult to coordinate, although their boundary is clearly defined by the understanding of the ray of solar consciousness. In order to carry out the plan in life, one must be ready with movability every hour.

How many times, having started out for Egypt, have We found Ourselves in Mongolia? How many times, having found a manuscript, have We locked it up again? How many times, having begun to erect walls, have We reduced them to rubble? How many times, having turned the steed homeward, have We again rushed it into the darkness of the night, lest, by sleeping overnight at home, We should deprive the plan of immutability? The seeming changeableness is no more than the vibration of life. The ways to the guideposts of immutability vibrate and billow like waves.

Affirming the plan, Our whole being is ready for the shortest way. Having just donned European attire, We are ready to fetch out the Mongolian kaftan. Having just decided upon a dwelling place, We are ready to depart. Such mobility can be born only from the realization of the immutability of the plan.

Our way is not that of an eternal wanderer but of a hastening messenger. The immutability of the plan illumines the consciousness with the manifestation of forces. We shall cross all the suspension bridges if the light of the plan is clear. One should so well understand the immutability of the plan that nothing can obscure it. That plan is immutable which is useful to all.

We do not see those to whom the plan of the New Country is not beneficial, and therefore we walk with sharpsightedness even in the darkness. If the teacher says: "Rush across a current!"—it means that the footing is foreseen, but let the foot not miss the stone.

One will start to build a bridge, the second will hire a swimmer, the third will sit down to await shallow water, but one will be found who will weave the silver thread of the spirit and cross upon it without the burden of the body, because I will take his load upon Myself.

Thus, under one roof live immutability and movability—two sisters of achievement.

A beautiful striving brings one to the Highest Light.

186. He Who has comprehended all creeds, Who has abided in all nations, decrees:

"I will allot to everyone according to his growth. Each one will weave his own purse. Each one who is afraid will have to account to Me. A smile to My enemy will be turned into a grimace, for you must leave My enemies to Me.

"He who thinks falsely about his brother will tie a heavy weight to his own foot. Weeds will make the spirit torpid. I cannot scatter goldpieces into nettle. To grow a garden of offenses is no great honor. The one who perceives the better will reap the richer harvest.

"To those who have encountered and to those who have responded I say: Leave to Me My sorrow and My joy about you. By the power of Christ, by the power of Buddha, by the power of the Messiah, proclaimed by the prophets of Truth, set up the scales.

"Show Us all that is great, and be ashamed of the

small worm that ruins the correctness of weight. The one who gives can receive.

"Reckon how much each one has given. Let us count accurately. On the left: fear, self-love, greediness, suspicion, demeaning, self-pity, misinterpretation of the Teaching, dusty whispering, treason in deed and thought. On the right: giving, compassion for others, daring, fearlessness, devotion, firmness, vigilance, movability, realization of the Shield, the path and light of achievement, adornment of the temple of the spirit, righteousness of understanding, exaltation of the good. On the left—loss and payment. On the right—the receiving.

"Each one will apportion for himself, for We see and hear. There is neither day nor night, and the messenger already saddles his steed.

"I send to you My achievement, affirmed by centuries. Keep the key to it clean." Proclaim this.

187. The Parable about the Asking One.

Dgul Nor was considered most wise. He had the good fortune to find a Teacher who came from the Sacred Subterranean Country but who was bereft of his tongue and his right hand. The pupil, constantly aspiring, asked a question, and the Teacher nodded. The pupil asked two questions and the Teacher nodded twice. Soon the pupil was asking incessant questions, and the Teacher unceasingly nodded. For three years the questions continued and for three years the Teacher nodded.

"Then, in Thy experience, everything is possible?"

And the Teacher not only nodded but bowed to the ground, and, opening his garment at the breast, revealed upon his bosom the image of the Blessed One bestowing with both hands.

Thus was wisdom affirmed and the creation of life exalted.

Verily, in a single sigh we cognize Space. And no word can convey the Infinite, and no thought can comprise the Light.

But at sunrise, facing the sun and receiving the ray into the solar plexus, one can feel the victory over the ocean, because through light one can touch the light of the spirit. But this consciousness is only in that spirit which can say: "I have renounced all in order to receive all." Thus, it is not a denial but an affirmation which has above it the Hand of Buddha.

188. The flights of the subtle body can be of two kinds; either it flows out of the feet and aimlessly wanders, or it passes through the upper nerve centers and flies upon spiritual missions. It is instantaneously transported across oceans, it teaches people, it imbues auras.

It must be said that only extraordinary strivings and resourcefulness impel the subtle body to concentrate the touch upon a physical object; because usually the spirit strives to act on spirit, overlooking the fact that objects can be excellent conductors.

Not only does the astral body act but also the mental body. Of course the astral body also emerges, but We do not value the actions of the astral body. We consider the consciousness of the mental body more important. To sharpen the point of this force is not so simple.

189. Two companions of Our works are joy and vigilance. If people could see the results of their discontent and could understand that slumbering is death, they would avoid the two chief coworkers of darkness. The evil sting of discontent penetrates even into the best places. A dull somnolence may becloud the head of a conqueror.

When you know the solicitude about you would you burn it by discontent, which has split great works and brought down the lightning upon the sender?

Remember, We have no discontented ones. Also no somnolence, with which the dark force besprinkles you.

Is there not ossification hidden in this poisonous effluvia? Slumbering is not Our sister. Those who have approached the Light will not pierce themselves with discontent, and will not turn to stone.

Slumber and such dusty manifestations should be avoided. The manifestation of the Shield should be treasured.

I shall repeat once again, but no more, because the Law forbids repeating to deaf ears.

190. Tell the new ones that the responsibility for thoughts has to be realized. Formerly, one was responsible for action; later the significance of the word was understood; and now it is time to know the conflagration of thought. It is better to learn silence and to purify one's thoughts.

Can the roar of a tiger possibly be worse than treacherous thinking? Not only for its actions but also for its thinking does humanity accumulate a grave karma. Thought inflicts tortures on the spirit, for there is no difference between word and thought.

A fool is he who will take this warning for a threat. There is no threat—We have only examples, and cares. Each one is free to jump into the abyss, but he must be forewarned.

I consider that now there is no need to repeat more about the significance of thought.

Although the time is sordid we had better think about the future.

191. Each one will apportion for himself. From the best plan there can be made a chicken coop.

Apportioning gold and silver is not Our occupation. One has to forget all conditions—then the light is lit. Every joyous loss is an immense gain.

The daring of despair is self-abnegation. But the highest daring does not expect any reward. And despair expects no reward. In Our language despair is the designation of a limit. An achievement is near to this limit. To the house where it abides one can screw an iron bolt.

I am knocking in the rain. Why do people fear only lightning? Sometimes a beggar's bag warrants a greater fear.

192. Cryptogram about Christ:

Night fell. Christ was seated at a threshold

A scribe approached and asked: "Why dost thou sit in the passageway?"

Christ answered: "Because I am the threshold of the Spirit. If thou wouldst pass, pass through Me."

Another scribe asked: "Can it be that the Son of David sits at the place for dogs?"

Christ answered: "Verily, thou defamest David, My Father."

It became dark, and a third scribe asked: "Why sitteth thou as if fearful of thy house?"

Christ answered: "I await the night's darkness, to free Me from sight of thee. Verily, let darkness depart into darkness."

Then, rising and pointing to Mount Moriah, whereon stood the Temple, He said: "My Grandfather created the Temple of stone, but He sits under the linen of the tent."

Said the scribe: "Madman, he believes that Solomon still lives."

And they departed in ignorance.

Afterwards Mary came out of the house and seeing Christ, said: "Teacher, share our evening meal."

Christ answered: "The gift of the heart glows in the darkness."

193. Cryptogram about Christ:

A member of the Sanhedrim asked Christ, "Wouldst thou come to us if we should call thee?"

Christ answered: "Better had I go to the cemetery, for there there is no lie."

The member of the Sanhedrim continued: "Why dost thou not acknowledge us when even thy father was married by one of our members?"

"Wait until your house crumbles, then shall We come."

"Wherefore shalt thou come, to destroy or to build?"

"Neither for destruction nor erection but for purification, because I shall not return to the old hearth."

"Then dost thou not respect thy forefathers?"

"New cups are given for the feast. Respecting a grandfather, one need not drink out of his cup."

194. Parables of Buddha:

A shepherd beheld a man seated in meditation beneath a tree. Seating himself beside the man, he tried in emulation of him also to think. He began to count his sheep and mentally to figure out the profit from the sale of the wool. Both sat silent.

Finally the shepherd said: "Lord, of what art thou thinking?"

"Of God," answered the man.

The shepherd asked: "Dost thou know of what I was thinking?"

"Also of God."

"Thou art mistaken. I thought of the profit from the sale of my wool."

"Verily, also of God. My God has nothing to barter,

but thy God must first go to the market. Perhaps on the way He may meet a robber who will help Him to return to this tree."

Thus spoke Gotama: "Go to the bazaar. Think faster in order to return quicker!"

On a ship traveled a trader of monkeys. In his leisure he taught the monkeys to imitate the sailors spreading their sails. A storm arose and the sailors hastened to lower the sails. The monkeys, knowing only how to spread them, followed the sailors and hoisted the sails again. The ship was lost because the teacher had foreseen only fair weather.

Thus spoke Buddha, the Restorer of the Lotus of Life.

195. You will ask why I speak against magic when I Myself am pointing out the cementing of the space, the significance of the influence of a circle, and other conditions which remind one of magic. But the difference is that magic seeks a substitute for life while We teach to ameliorate the existence by taking advantage of the possibilities of life itself.

196. It is well to point out: "Read again, and better, the old Decrees." I teach the new when the old has been put into practice. I teach the useful when the indicated and cognized cooperation has been accepted and entered into.

The best tinning takes place when the fire does not burn the ware. Success may be tinned only when its shell has been completed in spirit.

The hammer is working and the chains are clanking, and grey people continue to find pleasure in the cup of lechery. They do not know that the hands of the clock have moved imperceptibly and that tomorrow the doors will be closed to their ingenious amusements. My gatekeeper will tell them: "At dawn there was erected an altar to the Lord of Wisdom." And the grey ones will depart.

Stern and inflexible stand My guards. One cannot compare the steel of their helmets with the gold of the grey ones.

197. Separation precedes a meeting and a meeting precedes a separation. Therefore it is wiser to rejoice at separation.

A commandment to all warriors: When one leaves the ranks the others must proceed in the same direction. When the banner is flying the warriors do not desert. When the bonfires are ablaze the warriors do not push each other and try to take another's place. When the signal is given for a night march the warriors do not complain but march cautiously.

Before each manifestation you noticed a moment of seeming emptiness or cosmic silence. From small to great this moment is proportional. It is comprehensible that the physical world is very much on guard when letting through a spiritual discharge. Therefore, it is a difficult task to lead the physical world out of its inertia.

198. Our goal is not to be Teachers, but Co-Workers. But for this there is needed a firm realization that through mutuality absolutely everything will be brought to useful fruition. When signs of such allegiance are evident, then the mastery of the physical world is at hand.

In earthly churches people invoke Christ and wonder at His silence; whilst you perceive how one can resurrect Him amidst earthly life, without putting on a sackcloth and disturbing the space with discontent. Thus are the great Designs forged.

199. As different seas have different waves, so the space gravity must be held secure by various means.

Not through contents alone, but through application, much can be strengthened.

200. The most terrible statement is: "We have already attained." The Teacher Himself will never pronounce this destructive formula. We know the Plan, and We are tirelessly conceiving new details.

201. Why do I sense the mountain spirit? The Teacher is sending His Shield.

The Teacher wants to see you erecting a mountain.

The Teacher is yearning to see you disconcerted by nothing.

The Teacher feels how courageous you have to be to proceed.

The Teacher will point out when a grave danger is to be encountered.

The Teacher advises to keep courage ready.

The Teacher will help to conquer the evil hand.

The Teacher repeats not purposelessly the long-familiar thoughts.

The Teacher looks ahead.

The Teacher enjoins you to keep the spirit invincible.

The Teacher wishes to dispel fear.

The Teacher wants to make your judgment calm.

The Teacher restrains you from grievances.

The Teacher advises to plan bold projects as before.

The Teacher is concerned about your health.

The Teacher sends you forth.

The Teacher has warned enough.

202. Learning about sacrifice, you receive power. Success follows sacrifice. His Teaching is firmly grounded because it is based on sacrifice. Success is nothing else but the counterstroke of sacrifice. The success can be in advance of the sacrifice, as a loan, but inexorable is the fate of the debtor. If today one

can pay with little, within a year the payment due will increase. Before the year elapses the debtor becomes stooped with his burden.

I shall illustrate with a parable:

A man who had withheld the confession of a crime sat in prison. At home he had left riches which had come to him unexpectedly. The noise of every step outside suggested to him a pardon. He sent couriers to deliver the riches to the judge. But a simple confession would have freed him and preserved his wealth.

It is easier for a man to sit in prison than to pronounce the saving confession. When the judge is about to free one he must hear the redeeming "yes"—the desire to give up.

203. About the circles of keen sight and hearing. The first circle concerns the near ones and future events. The second is confined to current matters and to the near future. The third embraces the past which concerns the near ones. The fourth encompasses past events. The fifth is within the limits of the contemporary world. The sixth reveals the future of the world currents. The seventh contains all signs.

One can be strong in the first circle without being able to grasp the next one. Therefore, it is better to develop the seventh circle, because all manifestations are accessible to it but without personal gravitative influence—without limitation by the personal, narrower, sphere. It is better when, following a personal sign, one can receive signs about coming events of nations, or glimpses of a cosmic order.

One must know that amidst spirituality the realization of beauty lives but rarely. A sound understanding of beauty is the rarest quality, and will be valued by the Lords above many things.

It is better to approach the great with difficulty than to master the small with ease.

By a series of historical examples We will show the path of evolution.

204. In ancient cults there was a period called "the condition of opened treasures," when the priestess was already abiding on the eighth floor, entrance to which was prohibited, and the stairs were covered with the skins of leopards in order that no sound might penetrate. This state of "opened treasures" was so reverenced that the violation of the repose was punished as a religious offense.

Everything inharmonious is especially harmful; therefore, a thunderclap is less dangerous than the scream of a newborn. This simple truth was never written down. It is absolutely impossible theoretically to draw a demarcation line of harmony, because the tonality of the accord of spirituality is an individual one.

The ancients knew that the "treasures" are unrepeatable, and took measures against accidents. During the opening of the treasures the Elder of the Temple observed which of a gamut of sounds had the greatest effect. Each sound was accompanied by a definite color—thus were the conditions for each case determined.

205. A smile of determination is the best guide. One must acknowledge the goal and devote oneself to the plan of the Teacher.

Every personal desire is harmful, but striving toward achievement is required. Desire is not an achievement. Achievement is the realization of necessity. Desire can grow; a desire can be renounced or modified. The torrent is rushing on not because of its own desire, but because of an inevitability born of necessity.

The spirit knows where is the impulse of desire and

where the rock of necessity. I see the torrent of truth rushing on, and nothing can impede its course.

How often a Name of the Lords pronounced with faith helps to create the bridge of succor!

We see much that is far from beautiful. When working with humanity one has to wash one's hands often.

When you feel weary do not always ascribe it to yourself, but remember the waves of world reaction.

Only through consciousness of utter urgency will you swim across.

The pattern of work of the dark ones is first to sow disbelief, then to saturate it with desires, then to inflate these into crimes and reap a double harvest.

Ponder upon how to be more intelligible to humanity.

Besides the sacred language We have a language of silence. The condemned language of refusal and negation tears the hem of the garment.

206. Turning to the right, be ready to go to the left; nearing the shore, be ready to sail again; because every Command is for the good and for acceleration. In tense stillness hold your breath, for steps may resound.

Better a few annoyances but then the approach of the events. Better a short fatigue but then the near approach to the Teacher. Better wearisome journeys but then the approach to the Teacher. Better a sinking into dust but then the purification of the spirit. Better the rejection of conventional measures but then the obtainment of Light. Better grief about a Ray but then the Light of Christ. Better to give to others but then the lofty ecstasy of the spirit. Better to subordinate the spirit to the Command but then to reach the Teacher Himself. Verily, know how to guard and preserve.

When you feel a wondrous fairy tale, then does your spirit speak the truth. And when you draw the line of future life, Our Mirror shines. And when you count the parts of the world, Our Banner flutters. And when you look into the distance with an eagle eye, the light knocks at My Tower.

Thus, when you think about possession in common, or about the healing of humanity, We feel wings.

Expel small thoughts, they are stifling to Us.

207. In a card game you may receive the best cards but it is up to you to make the best use of them.

I am speaking about the pictures of the future. In conformity with quality of auras, these pictures are real and extend in a definite direction.

True, ill will can push the traveler into a different direction, and then he will see signs of a different nature.

Therefore, when receiving the pictures of the future it is very important to remember under what condition of spirit they are given. To the ray is given the corresponding possibility; otherwise justice would be violated. One should also understand dates similarly.

For cosmic dates manifested "vessels" are chosen, and they carry a chain of coworkers. Therefore, the substitution of coworkers takes place according to the request of the chosen ones.

If We notice the lameness of a coworker, We still do not replace him without the expressed desire of the elders. But if the spirit of the chosen ones recognizes a treason toward the work, then let them address Us, saying, "Thou, Our Sponsor, Who have given pledge, replace the coworker." This will mean that a link of the chain will be unlocked, and the consciousness of the chosen ones will be freed from the effects of the aura of the departing one. But the departing one takes upon himself his own fate, for everyone is free to build his own house.

We can summon, We can reveal pictures showing the expedient direction, but the application of Our Call is left to the free will.

Only devotion and understanding of the wisdom of the Plan insure the reality of the pictures of the future.

From the mountains distant vistas are seen, but the desire to crawl into a hole can only be deplored.

In times long past a debtor was cast into a pit called gehenna. Why crawl there of one's own free will? Thus, let us conclude about the vitality of dates and the mirrors of the future.

I wish to see everyone at his place and with greater understanding of achievement without expectation of personal gains. Is it possible to call a warrior who enters into the battle full of expectation of reward a hero?

Ages ago the Teacher Mohammed had to promise to the warriors of Islam raptures in Paradise. Will I have to promise the glitter of rubies? One must proceed without expectation; otherwise, deplorable is the waste of the time of eternal evolution.

208. Now let us conclude the law of co-measurement.

The builder must know how much load the pillars of the house can carry. From non-comeasurement results destruction, blasphemy, lie, treason, and many other ugly manifestations.

Can a building endure wherein to a flea are attributed the qualities of a giant; wherein a poker is sought more than the Lord; wherein the whirlwind is being compared to a mosquito's flight?

The condition of the Brotherhood is full co-measurement of thought and expression—this is the bulwark of the truth of beauty. To go through life with neither reticence nor exaggeration is easy. We sharply observe Our coworkers, for they should express themselves in conformity with the true meaning. Only thus can different beings cooperate.

The best judgment will be founded upon beauty. It is ugly to say, "I shall put the giant into a little box," or, "The eagle soars like a hen."

How often are the best apparati destroyed by non-comeasurement, which, with a little attentiveness, is easy to avoid.

209. Reading the suggested books, you will find sparks. Place into one receptacle the fragments of reverence to Maitreya. Thus, over the face of the Earth I Myself have laid the chips of the One Stone. A new miracle will bring the nations together. Our Ray will expel doubt.

The bonds of achievement are similar to results of the work in a laboratory. The hand does not shake while measuring the experimental liquid, because the researcher knows that a spilled drop can blow up the house. Only faith and courage uphold the hand of the experimenter.

210. The Ray of Christ is just as scientific as the ray of the sun, but to the crowds the simple finding of an object is itself a miracle. Is the change of races a miracle? Is the coming of the Teacher a miracle? Is the appearance of Christ a miracle? Does one prophesy a miracle centuries ahead? A miracle violates harmony, whereas cosmic events only affirm evolution.

Dreams and visions also are not miracles but a thread of life; that is, a knowledge of what is impending, revealed to such an extent as not to infringe upon karma. If people could without prejudice accept dreams and consciousness, the path could be improved.

The manifestation of new images is often distortedly

reflected. The mirror either expands or contracts, as when a surface undulates from an unusual pressure.

One must cautiously consider the so-called nightmares; their meaning may be significant.

211. What I will say now is very important. The canon, "By thy God," is the higher, and this canon is the basis of the New World. Formerly one said: "And my spirit rejoiceth in God, my Savior." Now you will say: "And my spirit rejoiceth in God, thy savior."

Solemnly do I say that therein is salvation. "Long live thy God!" So you will say to everyone; and, exchanging Gods, you will walk to the One.

There where one might otherwise sink one can tread softly, if without negation. There where one could suffocate one can pass, by pronouncing "Thy God." There where matter is revered one can pass only by elevating the earthly matter into the Cosmos. Essentially, one should not have any attachment to Earth.

Why is there a legend about the descent of Christ into hell? The Teacher addressed the lower strata of the astral world, saying: "Why, by cherishing earthly thoughts, bind oneself eternally to Earth?" And many revolted in spirit and rose higher.

Thus, find the God of each one and exalt Him. One can understand it in mind, but it is more important that it be accepted in the smile of the spirit. When the most difficult becomes easy, like the flight of birds, then the stones themselves unite into a Dome, and Christ the Mason will appear to each one.

212. Synthesis of spirituality is the rarest gift; it alone kindles the light of the world. Nothing can be compared to the light of the world. The light burns, but its ray is being sought.

213. Do not make enemies. This is an enjoinment to all. Know your enemies, beware of them, stop their

actions, but bear no malice. And if the enemy comes of his own accord under your roof, give him warmth, because large is your roof and the newcomer shall not take your place. But if it is difficult to overcome a deep feeling, then cover it with the smile of Light.

The sentiment of old fictitious accounts is verily incommensurate with the Plan of the Lords. For if we put upon a scale the works in their original form and the fictions devised through the exertions of hatred, the latter will be the weightier.

In the name of co-measurement one must find a right place for people; otherwise, we might as well speak with the same intonation about the center of the planet and an ink spot.

A piece of music played in one tonality evokes distaste. Therefore, We bid you to understand the practicality of co-measurement. But if you notice a long conversation about an empty shell, arrest the attention of the speaker upon the impracticability of naught. With many people this discipline is indispensable.

Do not be afraid if you be called insane, for the path is open to you. Do not forget to praise the enemies.

Let us conclude about the enemies.

214. About the non-comeasurement of dates.

Along with a ocean wave small streamlets of events are given. Can one confuse a streamlet with an ocean? But upon Earth one always hurries to confuse the personal with the world-wide. As the hand feels the thickness of a fabric, so must the spirit discriminate the depth of the events. Do not be fascinated by the seeming magnitude of events; because among the basic nodes there may be motley phantoms, and the streamlets can temporarily change their beds.

An incidental moment, or silence, or indisposition, should not be attributed to the wave. Thus, if the traveler stops for rest on his way this does not mean that he has deviated from the path.

The manifestation of a nodal wave rises instantaneously, but before each wave the boat hesitates. The more sensitive boat will shudder the stronger, because the dust of the explosion already fills the atmosphere.

Therefore, the co-measurement of the dates and events must not be forgotten.

Acceleration of the current can especially affect the organism. The complexity of events sometimes even seems to sever the thread; but this is only temporary, while the organism digests a double portion of the world's course. The complexity of physical conditions can augment the physical sensations. One should not then overtire oneself, as the waves of the ocean augur an approaching change.

215. Acceleration, as well as retardation, proceeds in waves. Therefore, when perceiving a wave of acceleration one must succeed in casting into it as many seeds as possible.

216. The laws of appearance of Teachers coincide with the plan of the whole culture. Karma rolls up like a scroll, and signs of the departing earthly power begin to flash out.

For those who know the future it is hard to observe these departing flickers. Like yesterday stands tomorrow. And the step is measured not in feet but in three-year periods. Thus is obtained the stride of Giants, to whom it is not frightening to step over whole centuries. Thus does the psychology of the spirit reach the Earth.

For earthly shells each century is like a menace. But the bridge of the spirit bestows wings of truth.

To those overstriding the span of three years it sometimes seems that they do not live. A specially propelled aerostat sometimes seems to be motionless because its apparent inertia does not correspond to the surroundings.

217. He who carries the knowledge of the future can walk boldly even upon shaky stones.

Success is then when the consummation is beautiful. Success is then when one can set forth upon a new journey.

The wish is already a part of the fulfillment. Courageously advance to Light!

The parting is the forerunner of the meeting. And St. Sergius used to say: "You must depart, otherwise you cannot meet again."

218. I wish to recall the cult of the high priestesses. There was one group which was brought into an exalted state by means of chemical preparations; another by way of magnetic currents; and there were also low grades of conjurations and mechanical whirlings. Then began the inward concentration on the threshold of sleep or the concentration upon a brilliant object. The knowledge which came from within, without any apparent conditions, was considered the highest.

The path of the world evolution proceeding under your eyes requires different conditions, and the time is coming when psychic forces must be strongly restricted for the sake of the spirit. For the last decade the lower strata of nature have taken possession of the lower psychic manifestations to such an extent that a danger to evolution is arising.

You can progress not by the way of the lower strata of phantoms and encumbrances but through cooperation with the Higher Planes.

219. Now about the circles of receptivity. The circles of keen sight proceed centrifugally and those of receptivity proceed centripetally. From symbols

and dim outlines they advance spirally to sharp fact, to clair-call, clair-audience, clair-voyance, clair-understanding, clair-achievement, clair-knowledge.

One must understand that into the category of the call the fact does not enter, because in this category a precise action can be misunderstood and will only increase the danger.

I do not wish to imply anything demeaning about those who need the call, but a fact in their hands would be like a loaded gun given to one ignorant in handling weapons.

Of course the boundary of the call is quite relative, but when one can pass over to the circle of understanding We greatly rejoice.

Each circle is like a caravan. Of course a whole caravan carries more than a single horse; yet, on the other hand, a single horse can delay the whole movement. Shyness or misstep can upset the march. Therefore, the concepts of achievement and clair-achievement differ very distinctly. It is possible to check the flash of the achievement, but not the fire of clair-achievement.

The flame of clair-achievement may flicker from the effect of Cosmic vortices, but it cannot be removed from the head. You will understand why a symbol, as an identifying sign, is necessary up to a certain degree. Later on it becomes unbearable and begins to fall off like a husk.

Like the music of the spheres, the all-existing resounds along the ways of Boundlessness and Non-recurrence.

As a bird flutters and then flies, so does a word gush from Our Furnace, and afterwards it can only be confirmed. Occultly the first moment is more important than a repetition. But when one can catch the boiling of the Furnace, it glows more powerfully than a command.

220. I have already told you that the Mother of the World conceals Her Name. I have already shown you how the Mother of the World veils Her Face. I have already made mention about the Mother of Buddha and Christ.

Indeed it is time to point out that the one Mother of both Lords is not a symbol but a Great Manifestation of the Feminine Origin, in which is revealed the spiritual Mother of Christ and Buddha.

She it was Who taught and ordained Them for achievement.

From times immemorial the Mother of the World has sent forth to achievement. In the history of humanity, Her Hand traces an unbreakable thread.

On Sinai Her Voice rang out. She assumed the image of Kali. She was at the basis of the cult of Isis and Ishtar. After Atlantis, when a blow was inflicted upon the cult of the spirit, the Mother of the World began to weave a new thread, which will now begin to radiate. After Atlantis the Mother of the World veiled Her Face and forbade the pronouncement of Her Name until the hour of the constellations should strike. She has manifested Herself only partly; never has She manifested Herself on a planetary scale.

One may cite many examples when even high Magi left behind them unexpected consequences and a desire to find support in the lower strata of matter. Such perversion could be termed the channel of the intellect, and can arrest for a long time the communion with other worlds.

Now people mechanically search for the already spiritually predestined.

The Teaching of the Future Epoch will be re-union of the spirit and intellect.

The course of the planets permits the hastening of the communion between the worlds, and the development of the human spirit will proceed along new ways.

The luminaries permit the acceleration of the course of humanity.

221. Now, more about the Mother of the World.

The Mother is Beauty; the world is self-sacrifice. Precisely by these two fundamentals are the Gates opened.

The bridge between the planets, and the shortening of race cycles, rests upon these two fundamentals.

Why the path of gradual progress, if a single flash of illumination can lift one over the boundaries?

The one whose path is to a far-off world usually meets a messenger upon departure from Earth. The liberated one tells this messenger whether he prefers to embrace a new path or would return to help the Earth. Of course many prefer a new path, but there are some who decide to continue the path here.

Verily, it is better to wait awhile in the vegetable kingdom and by-pass insects. One can even avoid a whole planet.

222. Just now, during the grave days of the approach of Mars, when the lower past currents are disturbing, We think only about the future.

The unprecedented deviations of planets help the awakening of consciousness. The Space is becoming dense, and the ray of Mars will be drowned in the light of the Mother of the World.

223. Healer, tell the ailing ones that the use of wine diminishes by half their chances, that the use of narcotics takes away three quarters of their vitality. Certainly in My pharmacy there is no place for narcotics.

Before using My medicines one must spend three years amidst prana.

224. M∴ has left many magnets on Earth. Therefore, I say, My path is easy to walk. The work toward cooperation with highest planets demands that on these planets abide harmonized spirits in conscious work. Usually the quest is from below and the answer from above. The higher, the more unity.

The created state of Earth's isolation must end, and it must be finally brought into the predestined circle. Otherwise, not only the Earth but also Mars and Saturn will fall behind in development.

Why do only a few go to Jupiter, when the atmosphere of the Earth is so encumbered?

One wishes to say: "Dear travelers, look upward. And if instead of clinging to the illusions of Earth you wish to fly farther, then your wings will grow. Instead, you have encumbered by the same miserable hovels the whole astral plane. The same slander, the same illusory smoke, but you forget that your phantoms fume malodorously. The rays of the sun are dimmed by your feasts of dullness. Empty shells create empty shells."

But imagine if the ghosts were to strive toward the creation of a beautiful movement. Then the rays, instead of only being disinfectant, could be transformed into rays of enlightenment.

Actually, thought creates beyond the earthly limits. Therefore, learn to govern the thoughts.

225. For a consciously developed spirit the period of sojourn on the astral plane could be limited to the interval of forty days, but various earthly conditions have prolonged this time to an interminable period. The misery and grief of those who are carried away from Earth binds them thereto.

The best instance of this is found in the Biblical

legend about Lot. For a new life they walked out of the city, and only one condition was imposed upon them—not to look back. But the wife of Lot looked back, and bound herself to Earth.

Religion says: He who goes to his fathers will dwell with them; he who goes to the angels will dwell with them; and he who goes to God will dwell with Him. It means that he who has ordained for himself the utmost progress arrives at the best attainment. Therefore, the best bidding to the one who departs from Earth will be—"Hurry, without looking back."

What about the dear ones? But the higher you ascend, the better and closer you will see them. Of course, the cause of the delay is usually in the last remaining near ones. Therefore, the abbreviation of the sojourn on the astral plane depends upon a proper cooperation.

The higher up, the more pleasant the stay; and on the border of the mental plane the spirit can rest, because there the spirit is already subject to lofty attractions. But one must consciously avoid the lower strata. It is necessary that an explosive impulse of the consciousness propel the kernel of the spirit upward as far as possible. Therefore, the moment of transition is so important, for in it one may dispatch oneself to the higher strata. Once the lower strata are contacted, it is very difficult to rise afterwards.

If the condition of spirit permits, it is far better to use the last flash of the nerves' emanation for flight. Thus the lower strata will be more sparse. It is important to dissolve the atmosphere of the lower strata so that it will not press upon the Earth. Cooperation from above and below will give the speediest results.

Transition without consciousness has been correctly noted. It is easy to assist in this, if beforehand there be strengthened the desire for lofty flight. Then the emanation of the nerves acts almost automatically.

Very helpful are prayers about the "wandering of the soul." The one thing wrong in them is that they reiterate about rest, whereas it would be better to stress haste.

Everyone should read and remember this, for it will not only help the individual but also advance the world plan.

226. The manifestation of labor for the future will transform the present. If people would understand that only the future exists, cooperation would approach.

There are two kinds of knowledge—one expressed in words, the other an exact one realized by spirit but not to be put into words. One cannot even explain in words how this understanding arises, but it is truly wondrous.

Our experiments and flights bring straight-knowledge. And if the spirit's subtle body prevents its penetrating farther than certain spheres, the illumination of the spirit contacts the most distant radiations of the Cosmos.

It would be stupid and crude to try to transmit by rough words the Light of Knowledge. It would be as ridiculous as are the absurd conventional terms.

I can whisper one thing: that you, foreseeing the possibility of knowledge through the window of individual flights, are correct in revolting against its belittlement.

227. I consider that the miracle of nature-spirits can be explained. Their main property is elasticity. Their form depends upon the aspiratory conditions. Falling into the focus of human sight, they are sucked into human form. Men will see them in human shape and animals will see them as animals, because they have no shell.

I attest that whether the forms are fearful or beautiful depends upon the reflex of the nerves. The potentiality of the elements is such that it is always ready to respond to nerve reflexion and thus to doubly reinforce Our sending in a definite direction.

One should not think that the elemental spirits are Our brood. Their manifestation may be likened to the spark at the moment of contact with a tense reservoir of dynamite. The consciousness of this spark becomes kindled upon contact with the human spirit. Of course their grade varies, as does the intensity of the dynamite's energy.

One can evoke mechanically the intensity of this energy, but We are against this magic; because it disturbs the regularity of the waves of the elements and is full of repercussions. One can use this energy outside of the usual earthly conditions. The rays can bring the waves of elements into balance. Of course you also make use of them, but as long as this action is from spirit it is less dangerous.

It is easy to transform many factories into focuses of magic. True, it is difficult to transmit in ordinary words the cooperation of the elements. Thus, the dynamo and the conjured circle both have a scientific basis. However, people at present work so zealously in the mines of evil that it is inadvisable to give them access to close possibilities.

The collision of the two Principles is unavoidable, and the sooner the better.

228. The spirits of elements strive toward union with man. They undergo the development of consciousness in lower forms of elements, and rarely possible are cases of their growth up to the consciousness of man. Man, however, in extraordinary cases can bypass a whole planet. But, of course, in strict classification

one may place the bulk of the elemental spirits into the primary forms.

You know how varied are the evolutions. The understanding should be expanded.

One can devote a special discourse to the elements. This domain is very beautiful.

229. The path of construction is absorbing, but it can be vouched that the steps of self-denial will also bring joy. Precisely the beauty of Cosmos brings selflessness closer into the consciousness.

The feeling of Cosmic loneliness is but the realization of direct paths, as only in this consciousness can man fly into other worlds, helping others for their sake alone.

230. Let whirlwinds and waterspouts darken the air; amidst their dust gleams the generative silver which spiritualizes the colors of Earth.

During the pressure of turmoil distressful moments can occur, because the eruption of a whole part of the world is a mighty volcano.

Since ancient times, people have been advised at the hour of turmoil to repeat a short invocation and by rhythmic repetitions to repulse the wave of influences. Later, these measures deteriorated into the senseless repetition of religious words; nevertheless the principle remains sound. Sometimes our spirit demands certain reiterations or enumerations.

During the best periods of priesthood's reign the chosen words were: "Adonai," "Ishtar," "Alleluia," and "Aum." Also, the repetition of the alphabet or of figures was in use. Of course, actually the power is not in the words themselves but in the creation of waves.

The fact is that sometimes through the invocation of the spirit a useful wave can be created. But habits are like numbness, under which even a powerful remedy ceases to act.

Sometimes during vortices one can create one's own purifying wave. When a poisonous breath is about to touch one, it is best to exhale. Likewise, one can create by will power a protecting veil. During the Mystery rites the priestesses were so deeply enwrapped in an almost invisible veil that they ceased to hear and to see, as if the thread of existence had been severed. It was a kind of purification, in an atmosphere full of turmoil.

I am reminding you about the mystery of the protective wave, because it had its origin in Asia.

Humanity is in need of new ways, and the window into the Astral World must be open. The wise one feels cold upon the blasted Earth.

231. I have said, I say, and I will say, "Help build My Country." And remember this Our request not in warmth and abundance, but in the cold and in moments of hardship.

It has been told that there will be instances which require courage, that there will be sharp precipices which can be crossed only in the Name of the Teacher.

They will say, "It is warm by the fire." You will answer, "I hasten into the cold."

They will say, "Fine is the fur coat." You will answer, "Too long for walking."

They will say, "Close the eyes." You will answer, "Forbidden on watch."

You can cross the bridge with invincible strength, and at the moment of weariness remember Our request, for the Plan is as beautiful as the radiance of elements.

232. The elements are spacial substance, imponderable and immeasurable—semi-amorphous crystals in the aspect of the so-called elemental manifestations. The essence of the unmanifested spirit permeates the substance of space.

It is said of man that he is born and he dies. About the elemental spirit it can be said that it flashes and becomes extinct. Like an arrow, the consciousness of the manifested spirit pierces into the substance of the elements, and like a magnet it gathers the molten substance. The birth of an elemental spirit is conditioned by the contact of a manifested consciousness. Verily, boundless is cooperation!

The quality, appearance and dynamic force of the spirit depends upon the spirit of the creator. Therefore, evil thinking is condemned as the begetter of monstrosity. The force of consciousness produces a corresponding reflex in the substance of space. And the flared-up focuses of space remain close to him who created them. A mediocre consciousness will beget easily extinguishable sparks, but a potentially growing consciousness can create giants. It is a factory of good and evil; therefore, the quality of thought is so important.

Thus, We have hewed out a picture of the evolution of life of the space, and We can urge humanity to do better and not to besmirch the waves of the beautiful Light.

The spheres of the elements are of dazzling beauty, and besmirching them is like destroying a wonderful flower. I feel that the teaching of pure thoughts will penetrate into people's consciousness. The sower of thought gathers the harvest. Therefore, with the Mother of the World all-seeing cooperation is unavoidable. The state of the substance of the space, pierced by the combinations of new rays, permits the beginning of the New Era. All Good should be gathered.

233. The Blessed One told this parable about the Wheel of the Law:

To a skillful scribe there came an honorable man

who commissioned him to copy, upon an ample parchment the man supplied, an appeal to the Lord. Immediately afterward a man came with a request to copy a letter full of threats; and he also provided a parchment, urging that the work be finished quickly. In order to give this letter priority, the copyist changed the sequence and hurried with the second order, taking up the parchment of the first man in his haste. He of the threats was very pleased, and rushed away to pour out his venom.

Then the first customer returned and, looking at the parchment, said, "Where is the parchment I gave you?" On hearing what had occurred, he said, "The parchment for the prayers bore the blessing of fulfillment, whereas the parchment of threats was devoid of effectiveness. Unfaithful man, in violating the law of dates you have bereft of its power a prayer which could have aided the sick. But besides this you have brought into fulfillment threats which are full of unparalleled consequences. The labor of the Arhat in blessing my parchment is wasted. Wasted is the labor of the Arhat who stripped evil of its power. You have loosed upon the world a malicious curse which will inevitably react upon you yourself. You have pushed from the path the Wheel of the Law so that it will not lead you onward but will break your way."

Do not write laws upon a dead parchment which may be carried away by the first thief. Bear the laws in spirit, and the breath of Benevolence will carry before you the Wheel of the Law, illuminating your path. Such unreliability as that of the scribe may bring catastrophe upon the whole world.

234. My Ray manifests the sign of spirit and presages a fierce battle. One can conceive the New World as the destiny of the spirit; it can be recognized according to the importance of knowledge. The spring of the

spirit brings health. The years fly, carrying to the spirit a foothold. The spirit summons and transforms the sign of priesthood into spiritual wonderment before the destiny of man.

235. Friends! Place four stones into the foundation of your actions: First—Reverence of Hierarchy. Second—Realization of unity. Third—Realization of co-measurement. Fourth—Application of the canon, "By thy God."

For the affirmation of the First, evoke all your love. Recall from your childhood the best smiles, the brightest rays of the sun and the first song of the birds beneath the window.

For the Second, gird yourselves in the armor of the day, take up the weapons of your actions, and refresh your perception by a draught of cooling water.

For the Third, select in your workroom the longest vertical line and call it the dimensional scale of the Plan. Apply mentally all discontents, irritations and fatigues to the scale of the World Plan, and, upon comparing, you will not find even the smallest place for illusory moods.

For the Fourth, picture to yourself all the boundlessness of the stellar universe. Verily, Our Father has many abodes; which of them shall we stain? Recalling the given canon, imagine that out of a closed house you are coming into the light. Thus all that you need will come to you.

Inscribe upon the first stone *A Dove*; upon the second *A Warrior*; and upon the third *A Pillar*; upon the fourth *The Sun*.

236. You may have noted in My Words cryptic passages or separate words not clear for today. Remember, guidance is on condition that karma be not infringed upon.

The understanding of Good must prompt one how to put milestones along the road.

237. It is best to strive onward; everyone has his own path. It is useful to attune the organism for receptivity to the Teacher's Teaching. Our Ray is working constantly, but concentration of the spirit is necessary. It is best to seek the Teacher's Indications in various manifestations of life. It is good to be able to pray. Prayer, or spiritual communion, is the highest manifestation; but for this, mental refinement and spiritual strength are indispensable.

The knowledge of communion is dangerous and can involve the weakening of the organism, like narcotics.

238. People often lack discipline of spirit and a sense of co-measurement. The key to the next attainment is the most difficult step on the path. Therefore, many beginners consider the path of an Adept like galley slavery. Not a flattering opinion, but I prefer the austerity of the spirit's drive.

The despair of spiritual emptiness before the anointing was well known to the initiates into the mysteries of Isis. On the night of the anointment the neophyte was locked in a special chamber where he emptied the full chalice of despair and rent his garments, enduring a mortal anguish in spirit.

Before dawn he sank into a stupor, and at daybreak, when the sun illumined the pylons of the temple and the priests intoned the morning prayer, the High Priest unlocked the door, awakened the neophyte, and led him into a dazzling hall, where he received his new name and was reborn in exaltation of the spirit.

239. On certain steps a clean place is indispensable. Our Ashrams are distinguished by cleanliness. The hygiene of the spirit presupposes the hygiene of the body. Human emanations are harmful for a certain

aspect of spiritual life. Many of Us with a special sensitiveness cannot endure the emanations of the world.

Ritual ablutions must be understood both literally and symbolically. The highest and final act of all mysteries was distinguished by the absence of ritual. Often the Initiator said to the neophyte: "Here thou com'st to Me, armed with the Secret; but what can I give thee, when the crown of fulfillment is preserved within thyself. Sit down, open the last gates, and I in prayer will alleviate thy last ascension."

240. Let the best warriors of the Holy Grail assemble for the achievement. Above all joys is the smile of achievement. Smilingly, accept the baptism of achievement. Smilingly, pronounce the sternest command. The Teacher walks beside you. In the battle He will support your arm, and in the council will indicate the solution.

Everywhere guardians are walking behind you. Time flies—hurry to store up knowledge! Joyously accept the austerity of achievement.

241. Joyously quivers the air of the hour before dawn, the hour when Buddha cognized the greatness of Cosmos, and when the Lord Christ prayed in the Garden of Gethsemane.

242. Few are the workers. Man, in pursuit of the miraculous, has lost the Guiding Hand. Again We come into the world, Again We bring the testimony of spirit. Now We shall decide the victory in battle and in the laboratory of the scientist. Man will be in tremor when above him the sword will be raised and a voice will shout, "Awaken!" Austere is Our manifestation, and the barriers of the world will be destroyed. By fire will I manifest My envoys, because I Myself lead.

243. It is better to know human weakness than to be nurtured by the images created by weak thoughts.

The truth is distressing, but it is time to know that the world is peopled with shadows. Before a catastrophe there always walk shadows. The hammer is raised; and terrible is the dance of shadows who have forgotten the spirit!

Shadows who know not, shadows who are bereft, are not aware of the New World. I foresee that the enemy camp will fall. I see the gold of their attire growing dim. I see the temple of amusements becoming hateful. Radiant is Our way.

244. The human mechanism is complex—a special conscious evolution. From the moment of inception of consciousness there is no common evolution. All is constructed upon an infinite variety of species. General laws are established with difficulty. Even such basic and immutable laws as the law of perfection and the law of compensation cannot be expressed by a single formula.

Book statements are not so simple in practice, and only an especially enlightened mind can penetrate into the structure of the evolution of man. Many lances were broken upon this question, but one may ask for enlightenment.

245. Today it is difficult to picture the times of the fall of Alexandria. Better even not to recall the years of this transitory period. Horror seizes one at sight of the religious superstitions of that time. Origen walked upon the still hot coals of the Ancient World. Knowing the covenants of Jesus, he suffered on seeing the ignorance of the crowd. Knowing the sacraments of ancient mysteries, he suffered on seeing the non-comprehension of the oneness of the Source. Knowing the simplicity of the Teaching of Jesus, he suffered on seeing the erection of churches.

He labored alone, suffering from too great contradictions of his own spirit. Along with an unusual clarity and simplicity of spiritual cognition, he was endowed with an unusual complexity of the whole being. In himself Origen atoned for the tempest of the early days of Christianity. Being an apologist of knowledge, he was indignant at the decline of knowledge among the priesthood.

246. I repeat that the light-mindedness of the world is criminal. Is it possible they do not notice danger? The tongues of flame denote the approaching storm of the spirit, but people are unwilling to understand Our signal.

247. Events are thundering. I am endeavoring to restrain, to bridle the madness.

If you could see all the crimes being committed! But We will not allow the panther to leap out. Seekers of spirit shall receive the Guiding Hand. Seekers of knowledge shall receive instruction. Those in sorrow shall receive consolation. Those who raise the sword shall be stricken. The scoffing ones shall be banished. Those who caused evil shall be smitten down. Thus do I decree.

248. It is astounding how the world is going to ruin! The destroyers and the destroyed will be swept away. The new ones approach. From pure clean places will appear new ones: nomads and ploughmen, orphans and vagabonds, monks and convicts, scientists and singers—in short, all those strong in spirit.

A legion of its own kind with understanding of spirit.

But one should know that among rejected people there are real pearls. Accept everyone who comes to you and says a word about the spirit. Even in the hardened eyes of a brigand at times a thought of achievement gleams. And even a convict understands self-sacrifice when on watch.

I want to see your cohorts real abodes for strong spirits. Remember that Christ prayed among thieves and that Buddha revealed the sacrament to a brigand. Judge according to the eyes. Thus write it down.

249. Let us speak about the sensitive apparatus.

Imagine yourself a fine needle, of unusual sensitiveness, which reacts to all changes in the surroundings. The needle is connected with a special apparatus which formulates all surrounding currents. The needle vibrates to all currents, all sounds, all images, and the formulating apparatus records all receivings. The sensitiveness is such that even a thought is registered. For preciseness of the work there is needed a constancy of surroundings. A predominant current creates a state of constancy. It means that the apparatus is adapted to this current. If the current is changed, then often the apparatus even stops; especially if the currents are not harmonized.

250. I rejoice when you are imbued with the significance of the future. These are especially crucial times. In old prejudices a mountain of incomprehension is revealed. Obscure are the people's ways. Verily, only Our exertion can alter the course of events. Brutal habits have filled the leisure of mankind.

Christ taught compassion, yet trampled is the law of love. Gotama, called Buddha, besought courage and energy, yet His followers surrendered to laziness. Confucius taught about an orderly system of government, yet his followers have succumbed to bribery and corruption.

It is difficult to say which crime is the worse. Therefore, it is impossible to speak about nations; one can speak only about individuals. Indolence is dreadful and can border upon crime. It is difficult to see the consequences of laziness, but it transforms a man into an animal. I assert that it is one of the chief obstacles on the path. On the spiritual plane at times a murderer is more mobile. Also, bribery deprives a man of the confidence of the Brotherhood, because the treason of such people is great. Also, lack of compassion makes a man unfit for achievement, because such souls are lacking in courage.

251. Truly, the whole Universe consists of many varied origins. By "origin" I mean a series of basic elements. We call those elements primary which are to be found in a free state—that is, not having entered into any combination. One of the principal traits of the creative power is the necessity for combinations.

For Us the universal principle is the basic law of Cosmos, which can be only partially investigated. Of course this cognition is difficult, yet there are possibilities. Many of Us have cognized it spiritually, but it is impossible to express it by a general laboratory formula so long as there are uninvestigated cycles.

The play of the Cosmos is like the flashing of a many-faceted crystal. The mind is capable of grasping only one of these flashes of the crystal. This is not sad but joyous. Of course, butchers cannot transmit the whole subtlety of conceptions.

252. People will forget rest, and will begin to rave in their folly. There is too little imagination, too little understanding, too little knowledge, too little sense of co-measurement, no beauty, no achievement, no desire to renounce comfortable habits!

Be prepared also to see comical figures. One must know how to lead. One must, one must, one must!

If you but knew how often We have to praise sandpiles, calling them castles. Of course, We rejoice when the builder is aflame with enthusiasm at the praise and is ready to erect new piles. Keep this in mind.

253. Discipline is the beginning of everything.

254. Let us speak about Lord Buddha.

People do not realize the foundation of the Teaching of the Blessed One. The foundation is discipline. Spiritually and bodily the monk of the community was striving to hold on to the path. In the first years he endured a heavy probation. He was forbidden to kill himself with ascetic practices, but he was enjoined to conduct the battle under sole command of the spirit. Thus austerely did Buddha instruct His disciples. Verily, they knew joy only in spiritual battle; that is why the thorns of the path are spoken of.

Only when the will of the disciple had become leonine, and a silver bridle of the spirit gleamed upon the feelings of the pupil, only then did the Lord lift the veil slightly and assign a task. And then gradually the pupil was initiated into the mysteries of knowledge.

255. The Blessed One said: "Truth is the sole source of courage." The truth correctly understood is the most beautiful chapter of wisdom in the book of Cosmos.

256. Devachan is not an obligatory state. Devachan is like a reservoir of forces. The renewal of the spirit is achieved there. But many souls have a large store of strength and do not need it. They await the date for a new manifestation. Hence, it is important to grasp the true teaching about skandhas.

The law of dates is as important as the law of karma. The law of dates controls the combination of skandhas. The spirit can correct the deficiencies of the physical body. The controlling factor is spirit.

A prodigious memory does not exist; there is only the capacity to evoke facts and images.

The astral plane is still full of earthly possibilities, but further on the knowledge of the spirit predominates; so earthly consciousness exists only in the earthly shell. In the astral body, however, there is still the remnant of a personal consciousness. But this consciousness is not the knowledge of the spirit. Consciousness is only one combination of skandhas. It is a confined knowledge of the spirit. The knowledge of the spirit possesses clarity of conception but it can be actively manifested only when entering into a combination of skandhas and fecundating the consciousness of the given combination.

In so speaking, I have in mind spirits subject to karma and to the law of dates. The evolution of free spirits is a different one.

We shall now approach closer to the question of the influence of karma upon the substance of the spirit in other spheres. This is important to know, as one should comprehend the distinction between consciousness and spirit-knowledge.

257. I affirm that the diversity in the other spheres is great. Name a man and I will tell you his evolution, but to formulate a general law is almost impossible.

Pride in the spirit is a step toward achievement. If all men would be kings of spirit, the harm would be halved.

258. Now about dates.

The law of karma and the law of dates are like the double-faced Janus—one gives birth to the other. Karma bears the fruit of actions and calls forth the date of manifestation.

Take note that personal karma, group karma, and cosmic karma must be combined—then will the date be correct. Often the development of a personal karma draws after it the group karma. Some spirits are ruled entirely by karma, which means that the knowledge of the spirit is at a minimum and karma is the sole possibility of evolution.

259. New, new, new ones! There is no place for old ones in the new construction. Why address the old ones, when already the lightnings of a new world illumine the horizon? When the traveler spurs his steed to reach his goal, and even We watch the clock of evolution! Putting an ear to the sands of the desert, We hear far-off voices which speak about an unprecedented Epoch.

260. There is no permanency in Cosmos; even a simple object in two consecutive moments appears different.

261. Of course one's own canoe, though full of holes, is better than another's ship. We value sailing only in one's own boat.

262. Certainly life is beautiful. But heretofore it was judged by animal instinct, and that is why the beauty of life could not be pointed out.

Egypt was of lofty culture, but it cannot be said that the present culture is lower. Culture used to be centered in the north of India, but only a limited class of people possessed knowledge. Castes—foolish mustiness—have hindered culture. Indeed, the Lord Buddha wished to abolish this caste foolishness. The Teaching of the Lord was imbued with joy.

263. Verily, Lord Buddha could manifest Himself. The Lord appeared to many, but He wished to make His Teaching the only source, and therefore He ceased personal manifestations.

Worship had no place in the Teaching of the Lord; its essence was knowledge and personal achievement. Just this was the characteristic trait of the Teaching of the Lord. Precisely because of this, His symbol was the lion. We often call the Lord, "King of Thought."

You have understood correctly about the unreality of the surrounding world. When I told you to proceed by the upper path of life, I was repeating the words of the Lord. As you see, the Lord recognized the reality of the surrounding world for the present cycle and taught duty to His disciples.

264. Close tightly your visors. On the verge of events there is silence. On the eve of battle quietly make ready your weapons. Whereas formerly one crossed the cities amidst the shouts of the people, now we shall pass silently, at dawn. Whereas formerly salutes thundered, now is the time of achievement.

We suffocate from people's worship.

Benevolence and austerity are one and the same concept. Formerly We sent the olive branch of peace. Formerly the dove was Our symbol; now it is the chalice of achievement.

Yes, each age has its symbol.

265. The epoch of individual trading has passed. Petty plunderers shall cease to exist. It is better to think about the welfare of the people.

I do not like to talk about reward for labor, but the remuneration will not be delayed. I speak of the joy of labor. The cooperative system is the sole salvation.

266. Value an expanse of thought. I teach you to esteem giants of will. Roundabout you I will bind the Sacred Knot—an invisible one. Our Decree is that you take on your shoulders the attestation to My Advent. Raise the weighty Shield with a firm will of consciousness. Let us say: "Lord, I will help Thy Country; my spirit is arrayed in the armor of fearlessness. Brightly glows Thy star upon my shield. I will catch on the shield all the arrows of Thy adversaries. I wish to help Thee."

267. I shall tell you about two of Akbar's commanders.

One of them received most explicit indications;

the other most fragmentary ones only. Finally the latter addressed Akbar, saying: "Why have I not deserved explicit commands, when I brought so many victories?" Akbar replied: "Thy understanding restrained the flow of words. Let each moment saved by thee be commemorated with a most precious pearl."

Thus, great is the joy of those who can understand the saving of a draught of the Source.

One can compare the essence of the Teaching with the exigency of certain moments of battle. I will not conceal from you that after a success dark rumors always leak through, and one should allow time for the dark missiles to fly by, especially when the fortress has been marked upon the enemy's map. But when the shells furrow the surrounding ground, it will be only the more fitting for future foundations. Therefore, he who has patience will be able to lay the future foundations. When we sit in silence the bond becomes stronger.

The manifestation of new growth denotes a new step, and we already know refined enemies. But behind us new forces are called forth, and therefore we do not need old ways.

268. The main mistake is that the questions and demands of life have not been formulated; whereas any moment I may ask, and what has been lost is not repeated. It has been said; "You know not the day, nor the hour."

I urge you to sharpen thought like a sword. One can learn endlessly.

When I entreat you to help build My Country, I do not address skeletons, but living, creating spirits. To each one is assigned his sacrifice. The symbol of the open eyes is so important.

269. Help to build My Country. People are loath

to see the trembling of the old world. Not sternness, but solicitude about the wonderful Plan impels Me to repeat over and over. And why make a lentil stew out of Amrita?

Every hour repeat to yourself: "Nothing will hinder my race to the Teacher. I have a thousand eyes, and my strength grows only in mobility." The manifestations of mobility and resourcefulness are inseparable.

270. You already know about the conjured circle, you know about its scientific significance. The Plan has that particularity that it has been decided to smooth away the protection of the circle, because it is a cosmic obstacle.

A kind of fear has girdled humanity with various artificial circles. Now it is time to put aside conventional formulae. It is time to meet with awakened spirit the manifestation of Earth and Heaven. It is time with open eyes to tell to the brood of the elements: "I do not fear you! You cannot impede the way pointed out to me."

It is time to say to the Light: "I come as thy helper, and to the sun itself I will stretch out my hand. And as long as the silver thread is intact, the stars themselves shall be my armor." Thus simple is the way ordained to man. And finally the idolatry of symbols will be erased by the ray of Light. And We shall be permitted to be not Gods but Co-Workers. This is the covenant of simplicity.

271. Be not afraid to examine closely the armor of your brother. Only by fingering with a careful hand all the links of the coat of mail can you recognize which side of the brother is the least defended. An armor that shines from the outside may not withstand even a light arrow.

Therefore, if you detect a weak link you can say:

"Brother, in the Name of the Teacher, examine thy coat of mail and finish its tempering; otherwise it is better to fight without any armor at all!"

Therefore, examine the weapons before each battle. Cruel is the lot of him who holds a hilt only.

We rejoice especially when the magnitude of the Plan is being garbed in simplicity. Remember, simplicity possesses the power of attraction. This magnet corresponds to the new abode.

The horned thinking does not permit birds to sing, but My march is only with a song.

272. They will ask: "What kind of heaven is yours?" Answer: "The heaven of toil and struggle." Out of toil is born invincibility; out of struggle, beauty.

Yes, even today I said that I Myself come! Indeed My arrows fly into My Country, and multicolored sprouts await the gardeners.

Upon the walls are My signs, and in the whisper is My breath. Let the bushes grow wild, it is easier to remove than to plant. Fear nothing, for, though Our flowers are multiform, by the Voice of the Lords you shall bring them into order.

Notice how Our field is overgrown. Useful sprouts are yet green, dry ones fall off and become black. One can already draw a chart of the new conflict. You will add regions of the struggle of spirit and blot out the mountains of former pride.

As I have said, it is better with ragamuffins than with hypocrites. Become accustomed to perceiving the fire of spirit in the eyes.

The swallow-tailed coat is devoid of the star of struggle which shines on the kaftans.

Today let us remember the Heaven of toil and struggle.

273. Together with co-measurement, necessity must be understood. The final test will be that of

necessity. In other words, each one being tested must say what it is that he considers most urgent. According to the quality of the immediate reply will his consciousness be measured.

274. The degree of usefulness can change. The grades of usefulness are as numerous as leaves upon a tree.

If we long for an undeferred Advent, then the ways should be cleared without delay. Day and night must one be accustomed to fulfilling the Decrees and being imbued with the Covenants.

I dislike all bigotry. Let the Ray illumine achievement. Whither shall I send the Ray, if there is wet muslin instead of a shield? Foremost are promptness and firmness of the hand in striking.

As I send you each shield, so must you make use of each moment. Not for a reward and not because of fear do you go forward, but because of a realization of the Cosmic beauty.

275. I will tell you of the origin of the controversy between Buddha and Devadatta.

Devadatta asked: "Wherefrom is each action begun?" The Blessed One answered: "From the most necessary; because each moment contains its necessity, and this is called the justice of action." Devadatta persisted: "How is the evidence of necessity ascertained?" The Blessed One answered: "The thread of necessity crosses all worlds, but whoever has failed to realize this remains within a dangerous chasm, unsheltered from the stones."

Thus, Devadatta could not distinguish the line of necessity, and this obscurity impeded his way.

A spirited steed even with the end of his hoof feels on which stone to step next. So is felt the order of mobility, co-measurement and necessity.

Many of Our historic records are taken for inscriptions of ancient lawgivers. Often the name of Christ or Buddha even impedes the ease of acceptance, but characters on an unknown stone more readily attract serious attention.

Must one explain that the best result is when the spark of the spirit flashes out? Therefore, know when it is better to remind of the Name and when more useful to give the substance of the Covenant. Remember, when you will be upon different paths.

276. Let us send seven servants to the market to bring some grapes.

What do I see? The first has lost the money. The second has exchanged it for intoxicant wine. The third has hidden it. The fourth did not notice that the grapes were unripe. The fifth, testing their ripeness, crushed the entire cluster. The sixth chose wisely, but brushed them loose and scattered them through carelessness. The seventh brought a ripe branch and even found leaves to adorn it.

Thus seven passed along one road and at the same time.

Maintain the statute of the New World. We will bring together spirit and body, for there has been no achievement more beautiful. I consider that we are living through a most complex time. Reflexes of events are crowded against the gates.

You know how a ship rushes forward on a wave. Therefore, verily, one should nurture not the hearing but the spirit.

277. About the laying of magnets.

The magnet forges the projection of the evolution of the planet. The magnet manifests immutability. The magnet affirms the path of humanity. There are several aspects to the magnet: either the unsplit body of the leading planet; or a part of that body, connected with other parts; or an extraneous object which has acquired a link with the magnet through contact. The magnet either remains invisible, attracting the flow of events; or it serves as a center of conscious action; or it enlightens the man who found it.

One can trace in the history of humanity a network of magnets, which have flashed forth like guiding fires.

How then does a magnet work? It transmutes into action the ideas of space. Many magnets are lying under the foundations of cities. Many have been discovered.

I repeat that the symbol of diamonds in a meteor sent from outer space must be understood scientifically.

One must gather up all the minutes of morning and evening. The life of the denizen is ended; the dawn of an achievement has begun. Destiny is ready to account for all burdens, but accept them.

A ray can shine in through a window.

278. The quality of being invisible is often a salving one. The quality of being silent is often a salving one. The status of being the keepers of secrets is honorable. The position of being entrusted is honorable. The power of aspiration helps the growth of spirit.

279. I consider that all signals must be lit up, so that the signs may be easily understood. To each of the summoned ones I will give signs, but these must be accepted. I can say that at times one has to resort to excessive signs, but they cannot always be made use of.

Let Me recall: Once We succeeded in saving a man from a fire, but he did not harken to the signs and broke his leg. At another time, to save someone from penning a disastrous signature, there had to be applied, besides spiritual influence, such a muscular force that his hand became numb for a long time. In order that a man be saved from a dangerous beast he had to be pushed off a footpath. Hence, one should not compel the use of extraordinary measures, and one must sensibly harken to the saving signs.

280. A spiritual uplift must be bestowed. We reverence the Teacher in action. We live aspiring to a wondrous vision. Our road is strewn with horseshoes of achievement. Above Our tents shine the rays of valor. Our joy is to be singed by the flame of Truth. Our way is triply lengthened. Is it not a joy to strive against lifeless matter, and to kindle the sparks of creative spirit with the lance of spirit, by displaying activity?

Teacher, Teacher, Teacher, walks holding the arrow of Command. Never will I choose a calm surface of water; rather will I accept all thunderings, and My Scrolls, as lightnings, will transform the Dome of the Universe. I will send a dove as messenger but I will descend as the Eagle!

Thus, let each of My warriors prepare his armor!

281. You already know about the two commanders of Akbar—let us add something about a third. This one asked: "Why are tardiness and prematurity equally condemned?" Akbar replied: "My friend, there are no equal values. Hence, if the prematurity embraces resourcefulness its merit is the greater, because tardiness is linked only with death. Prematurity is to be adjudged, but tardiness is already condemned."

282. My Command is that you understand the importance of what is happening. As I promised to issue today a Decree, so be you ready for action.

If I see that one should go by camel, go!

If I see that one should fly, fly!

If I see that one should sail, set sail!

If I see that one should creep into a burrow, creep!

If I see that one should appear by midnight, appear there!

If I see that one should arrive before dawn, be on time!

If I see that one should cover the Shrine with a shield, cover it!

If I see that one should not fall asleep, do not slumber!

If I see that you must trust Me, trust!

And let your mantram be: "I will help to build Thy Country, in the Name of the Mother of the World, and of My Father!"

Let us increase our strength by the fire of readiness; and we shall walk upon golden sands, because we are going to the Lords.

283. You may proclaim My desire to see all at work.

One must exert one's aura; it cannot grow otherwise. It should be clearly understood how useless the heavenly rays are if they are not met by the emanations from the nerve centers. I have already spoken about numbness of the tongue and broken arms as the result of heavenly action without earthly response.

284. I wish to see cooperation not on paper and in assurances, but in action. It is right not to speak about love but to show it in action. It is correct to abolish assurances of devotion, for it is manifested in action. It is correct not to utter superfluous words, as they are needed in action. It is deplorable if during an assault the warriors break ranks and begin to assure the leader of their love. Verily, the current time is one of assault, and each stone must be taken by an adroit move. Aim the arrows skillfully.

I have spoken from the very beginning about the ineffectualness of rays when there is non-correlation of emanations. Fatigue and irritation can deprive one of an urgent message. One must know how to reach Us over and above one's sensations.

285. Thus, after Cosmic designs let us turn to the carrying of stones, and on each We shall inscribe the symbol of the cross. I shall remind you how Buddha selected disciples for an achievement.

During work, when fatigue already possessed the disciples, Buddha would ask the most unexpected question and await the promptest reply. Or, placing the simplest object before them, He would suggest that they describe it in not more than three words or not less than one hundred pages. Or, placing a pupil before a locked door, He would ask: "How will you open it?" Or, summoning musicians beneath the window, He would have them sing hymns of entirely dissimilar contents. Or, noting the presence of an annoying fly, He would ask the pupil to repeat some words unexpectedly pronounced. Or, passing in front of the pupils, He would ask them how many times He had done so. Or noticing a fear of animals or of natural phenomena, He would give them the task of mastering it.

Thus did the Mighty Lion temper the blade of the spirit.

Remember and apply!

286. The Ushas of the New Dawn may now be manifested. Already the power of Light is consuming the darkness. M∴ is an invincible Spirit.

My Spirit knows how the power is being forged. I advise not to pray to Me but to invoke Me. And My Hand will not delay in manifesting Itself in the battle.

How did we cross deserts? How could We avoid black arrows? How could We bestride untamed steeds? How could We sleep under the same tent with a traitor? How were We able to better Our lot while facing the fire of feather-grass of the desert? How did We conquer the stones of the torrent? How could We find the way in the night's darkness? How could We comprehend obscure wishes? How did We discover the path of life? Verily, by vigilance of the spirit.

Every moment We are ready to give the bread of life to him who will choose the same path of vigilance of the spirit. My Ray can illumine the actions of the spirit.

To My Ray respond the beings who have clothed themselves in the protective purple of valor. Where there is the dusty mould of fear, there the glaive of the Ray is turned into a whip!

287. Know how difficult it is to reach the hearts of people. The spirit does not pierce through, and the carnal envelope is becoming dense. How much more, then, should one welcome those who look around like eagles, and to whom the mist of the future is like a clear mirror.

Although the events of the conflict are great, still one thing I can promise to the faithful ones: in every situation We will safeguard their dignity. Those hostile currents We will turn into usefulness.

A Command to My warriors is not spoken twice. Let us build better our ways, marking the possibilities. Let us not be afraid if at first glance these possibilities appear too scattered. Grass does not grow instantaneously. But fortunately I see youthful heads worthy to be entrusted with the loosened strings.

You must rely upon the unknown ones and the Unseen Ones.

288. When people leave they feel one of two ways: either that they have lived long in this place, which means that their aura had become attached to objects, or that everything has come to an end around them, which means that their aura is surging in aspiration.

It is very important to distinguish these two kinds of people. Often by an external sign one can form an opinion about the fundamental category.

Who then are My people? Those who do not feel any place to be their home; those who do not attach any value to objects; who love to ascend mountains; who love the singing of birds; who value the air of the morning hour; who value action more than time; who understand flowers; who display fearlessness without noticing it; who abhor gossip; who esteem the manifestation of the joy of beauty; who understand the life beyond the limits of the visible; who feel when one can partake of Amrita; who hasten to fulfill the prophecy. These, My people, can use My Power.

As King in the Land of whirlwinds, I can send them a drop of dew from the tree Elgario, which reveals the life of the future.

289. Let Me tell you how a great warrior achieved one of his greatest victories. He set fire to the steppes behind his own troops and gave a thousand horses to the prisoners, offering them escape. In terror they rushed to his enemy and spread fear there. On their heels his hordes came rushing, seeing no other way out. Quicker than flames they trampled down the foe.

A short-sighted leader sets the fire behind the enemy forces, but the wise one kindles one behind his own.

Similarly, when the first wanderers from Asia were on the march they destroyed bridges and crossings behind them, so that retreat would not enter their minds.

290. There is an Oriental riddle: "What is it that likes to be buried?" Answer: "A seed."

Precisely, the seed of a plan must be buried in the ground, but when it begins to come to life it grows only upward.

The Teacher sees new possibilities, and the fire of the steppe chases the riders in one direction.

291. Amidst dusty daisies rises a lily of Heavenly Purple. It is better to live near the Celestial Flower, for earthly flowers are the sole living bond between Earth and Heaven.

In the creation of floral pollen there are precipitated, as it were, crystals of prana. Without frivolity one can say that in flowers the Heaven settles down upon Earth.

If the Earth were deprived of flowers, half of its vitality would disappear. Just as important is the snow, and like beacons of salvation stand the snowy mountains.

292. When the scope of the work grows, the floors and ceilings begin to crack. Men understand with great difficulty the difference between "it can be" and "it will be." It seems to them that if it can be it already will be. But where is the achievement and where the desire to pass over all walls?

293. Let us imagine the Earth crammed with wireless stations. But a few of them will be of very high tension. Only these few will direct the life of the planet. Exactly so do there exist spirits of high intensity who have fully charged their accumulators in past incarnations. Their characteristic feature will be a firm consciousness of the indissolubility of their inner ego, whence is born the concept of the higher freedom. And to the station of high tension is adjoined a network of smaller stations which receive its continuous waves. Thus does a spirit of high tension nourish its surroundings; it is analogous to a solitary tower reigning over the space. That is why people are attracted from early childhood to such magnets, even overburdening them.

Achievement is not renunciation; it is containment and movement. Thus, when I say, "he who has renounced," it should be understood as, "he who has contained." It is impossible to present the substance of renunciation, because beside it nestles prohibition. But containment emphasizes conscious understanding.

And how did the Great Mother renounce the worlds? In that She contained the greatness of the structure of the future, and henceforth nothing could hinder the growth of the spirit.

Loyalty is a quality of the spirit of high tension, and the evincing of containment makes true achievement a joyous acquisition. Thus can the achievement be developed, for a luminous attainment brings forward a following one.

Holy Heroes have been represented correctly as sailing in a boat. Thus does the wave of world energy carry along those who have entered its current.

Again one has to remember the difference between threat and solicitude. When I warned an illustrious horseman to learn how to jump off a speeding horse, he considered this contrary to the customs of his steppe country. But when a frenzied steed brought him abruptly to the shore of a rapid, he had to jump off awkwardly, and remained lame thereafter.

Yet it is easy to adhere to the world current through faithfulness. We are striving only toward joy.

294. Strive into the future, by-passing the soot of the present.

295. Learn this: One should not be destructive but should summon the best patience.

It is terrible to see how few are those who respond to the call without evasive excuses and complaints. One may give to men the most precious, but at the hour of the call they will forget all they have already received.

How can one think about the New World if the old one has not been realized? A hedgehog has many needles, but these will not make him a King.

Our mentioned Help can flourish when it is accepted by those to whom it is sent. We rejoice when the Hand is not rejected.

296. Do not live on income from money. This profit is stained. The best interchange of goods is by direct exchange of objects; or if necessary they can be allowed to be exchanged into money to be reconverted immediately.

Do not be displeased except with yourself. Do not let others do what you can do for yourself, and in this way you will abolish the thralldom of servants. Do not say twice what needs to be said once. Do not re-tread the same path, for even a stone threshold will wear away. Do not swim where one has to fly. Do not turn back where one should make haste. Do not distort your mouth in ill-speech where you should pass in silence. When the steel of achievement is needed, do not cover yourself with rays. No need for a saddle where wings are growing. Not the fist but the hammer drives in the nail. Not the bow but the arrow reaches the mark. Not by my God, but by thine. Do not be bounded by a fence but by the fire of thought.

297. Regard nothing as belonging to you; the easier for you not to damage things. Think how best to adorn each place; the surer will you protect yourself from rubbish. Consider how much better than the old must each new thing be; by this will you affirm the ladder of ascent. Think how beautiful is the morrow; thus will you learn to look forward. Think how cruel is the condition of animals; thus will you start to pity the lower. Reflect how small is the Earth; thus you will improve your understanding of relationships. Think

how beautiful is the sun hiding behind the Earth's sphere; thus will you restrain yourself from irritation. Think how white are the doves in the sun's ray; thus will you strengthen your hope. Think how blue is the sky; thus will you approach eternity. Think how black is darkness; thus will you guard yourself against the cold of retreat. Think courageously about the Images of the Great Ones; thus will you follow the line of unity. Think what happiness it is to walk upon the crust of the planet, imbuing it with the consciousness of the spirit. Think what happiness it is to walk under the rays of constellations, being a focal point of rays millenniums of years old. Think about Our Hand, which guides vigilantly; thus will you prolong the thread of life.

298. When someone bars your way, step aside in silence if you know your path. When you have to find shelter, find good words for the host. If your path is broad, when the hour of departure strikes, find good words for those remaining. When a tree blossoms by the roadside, do not break it; maybe it will give joy to those coming after you. When you hear a call of greeting, do not spoil it. When you hear a singing bird, do not shake the tree. When you see children approaching, say, "We have been expecting you." When you are hurrying for supper, step on dry stones. When you go to rest, set your thoughts in order. When you hear something pleasant about yourself, do not write it down in a note book. When you think about an offense, look back for the dust on the floor.

299. "It is better to accept an urgent message than to hide from the messenger. It is better not to paint brightly the gates on a dusty road. It is better to let one's horse into a vegetable garden than to make it step on stones. It is better to forgive a village policemen than to have a lawsuit with the magistrate. It is

better to give up carrots than to be deprived of peas. It is better to fall asleep on a wooden plank than on an ant hill. It is better to receive sound reprimands than to smirk at syrupy speech. It is better to be friends with a donkey than to listen to a fox. It is better to call a physician than to bleed a demon. It is better to shudder at the torments of the past than to be in doubt about the future. It is better to judge in the morning and forgive in the evening. It is better to think by day and fly by night." Thus is it said in the book "The Pearl of Dreams," written in China.

300. The Teaching of new possibilities of life attracts practical heads, and when the manifestation becomes possible it will be accepted as readily as telephotography. It is gratifying to realize that two worlds will unite under the very eyes of humanity. The condition of spiritual purity will be understood as a practical requisite in life. And again, as in the most ancient times of priesthood's prime but in a popular application, the fire of knowledge will begin to shine. The chief necessity is to bring into balance the forces of visible nature and the Power of the Invisible Sources.

It is easy to attune the apparatus of visible science with the conduits of the Higher World. For instance, clairaudience will be easily understood as the wireless telephone, which will be very soon established. But just then attention will be paid to the differences in the quality of communications, and in comparing the peculiarities of the mediators the practicability of spirituality will be understood.

As photography will never replace creativeness, so too a physical apparatus can never substitute for spirituality.

A special harm can be found in "phenomena," because the discharge of the forcibly disturbed matter produces a repelling atmosphere of tossing electrons. Nothing harms an organism so much as useless phenomena.

301. I rejoice to see how the lightning flashes of foresight regarding the people's welfare sparkle amidst your thoughts. These thoughts have to be launched into space. If you could daily spare half an hour for the future! Verily, the bonfire of your thoughts would receive Our welcome.

Let the things of everyday life vanish, but let the country of the future be embodied in thought. And what cleanses the spirit more thoroughly than the thoughts about the welfare of others? And what tempers the armor of steadfastness better than the wish to lead others to Light? And what weaves a better smile than a desire to see the very last child laughing? I urge you to think thus about the future, to place daily a pearl into the necklace of the Mother of the World. And so, concisely and simply think how to adorn the Hearth of the World.

There should be no comparison with the past, for a wrinkle of the past is usually a nest of errors. One can sail past alien shores; one has only to admire the world of light bestowed upon all that lives. Light is the best bridge between the visible and the Invisible.

When one can think about the future not by the evening fire but in the radiance of the sun, then the dew drops of prana illumine the thinking brow.

302. Let new countries also realize the power of the aspiration of the pure in heart. Let them understand that hypocrisy of thoughts is an obstacle to the attainment of communion in spirit.

Say to all who hope to be with Us that they should keep their thoughts pure. Achievement is born of pure thoughts. No display of action will yield fruit unless it has been uplifted by the wings of a rainbow thought.

I understand how difficult it is to catch the fleas of thinking. That is why I repeat: to ventilate the convolutions of your brain so that the tiny jumpers will have no chance to settle their progeny there. Chaotic thinking begets small insects and cuts off the best paths. Vermin of the body cause a man to be shunned. How much more repellent must be the vermin of spirit!

When thoughts flow broadly, then even their unpleasant direction may finally be not harmful. But when the thinking resembles in content a drop of stagnant water, then there is no possibility to reveal the image of the New World.

One must affirm one's thinking, and steadfastly keep in mind the four given precepts. One has to remember this; one must avoid confused thoughts. I strongly urge you to emphasize the beauty of the firmament and to link it with thoughts about the future.

303. The dates of nations' destinies can be cognized according to the waves of the understanding of religion. Where there is obvious unbelief, there the harvest of God is already near. But where there is hypocritical splendor, there the sword is ready. The example of Saul will be instructive.

Nowadays, on the day of an annual festival we understand how the most ragged vagabond can manifest an achievement, and how a chiton can conceal noisome ulcers. Thus we see a new dividing of the world. One can forgive ragamuffins much, but the blinding gold of sumptuous chambers cannot outweigh the chalice of justice.

304. I have already told you about the inner understanding of languages. Write down this legend:

It was once proclaimed that a certain high priestess could understand any language through the inner consciousness, and wonderful results followed. Envoys from far-off lands spoke to her in their own language and she understood them. Thus there was created a legend about the eternal language.

But crowds of people wished to be convinced about it. Many foreigners were brought forward, and the priestess was led down from the eighth floor in spite of her protests. But nothing was manifested for the people, and the strangers reiterated in vain their speeches.

Thus was ruined one of the best possibilities. Yet it would be possible to put this into practice by studying the quality of aura, because this is the bridge of both bliss and contagion.

The ability to understand even one's own native tongue depends not upon the ear but on the contact with other centers through the aura. Therefore, it is better to say, "I have understood," than to say, "I have heard."

Therefore, as to the question of aura, its color is not so important as is its inner intensity.

305. My Hand will not tire to lead, but you do have to walk, each one with full strength. It is correct to apply one's strength to the difficult, because everything easy is incommensurate with the future.

What does a mother say to her son upon his leaving for war? "Know how to defend thyself." Thus, My warriors also must understand how to fight single-handed.

The chain of the circle may facilitate, but resourcefulness is tested when one is left to oneself.

306. Seldom do We choose the water routes. The element of water is in opposition to the magnetism of the mountains. The arrows of the lightning pierce the water without accrual of results. But We strive to insulate each current.

Metals are to be selected not according to their

costliness but to their resistivity. One should not wear copper things. The ancients knew how much more useful was bronze. Also, zinc should no longer be used in the household. Not only is infection possible through contact with copper, but the channel of this metal brings maladies. Therefore, the copper coin has to be abolished. A tiniest silver one is better.

The crime of speculation has to be prosecuted relentlessly, because the Earth is sick from speculation.

Each epoch has its own plague. At present it is the epidemic of speculation. It must not be thought that humanity has always been plagued with this disease. But this disease brings promise of a radical change, because it cannot pass gradually and a paroxysm of evolution is needed in order to root out this infection.

307. Prayer is the realization of eternity. In prayer there is beauty, love, daring, courage, self-sacrifice, steadfastness, aspiration. But if in the prayer are included superstition, fear and doubt, then such an invocation is related to the times of fetishism.

How then should one pray? One can spend hours in aspiration, but there may be a prayer of lightning speed. Then instantaneously, without words, man places himself in continuity with the whole chain into the Infinite. Resolving to unite with the Infinite, man inhales emanations of the ether, as it were, and without mechanical repetitions establishes the best circuit for the current. Thus, in silence, without wasting time, one can receive a stream of refreshment.

Only developed spirituality can uplift the human consciousness in a single sigh. But We must repeat about prayer, because people will inquire about it.

Needless are conjurations, needless are entreaties, needless is the dust of humbleness, needless are threats, for we alone transport ourselves into the

143

far-off worlds, into the treasuries of possibilities and knowledge. We feel that they are predestined for us, and we approach them daringly.

Thus understand the Covenant: "Pray in no wise but in spirit."

308. If we begin to decompose matter, we see that the liberated atoms begin to arrange themselves according to the basic tone, and, escaping into the ether, they form a rainbow that resounds with the music of the spheres.

If an entire planet be decomposed, then indeed the result will be a rainbow. This can be observed in every dissolution of visible matter.

Our Ray dispatches myriads of purified atoms, which enwrap the man if there is no astral whirlwind around him. This is the reason for the calmness of the spirit, as otherwise the remnants of Karma will obscure the object of the sending.

The lower spirits rend the Ray like monkeys, tearing the precious fabric without any benefit to themselves, because the atoms of matter are useless for restless shells.

This must be remembered while uniting the spirit in prayer with the Infinite.

309. Keep now in mind that in time of danger you must encircle yourselves with a realization of personal invulnerability, and then send your consciousness to meet My Ray. Imagine mentally how your spark rushes to My current. Such reciprocity increases the current, and is excellent in time of fatigue. There may be various incidents on the path in which a reciprocal current will be especially useful. It is best to reinforce each possibility.

310. Surrounded and threatened, Akbar addressed

his commanders: "The less agitated is the substance, the more clear is the reflection of the summits."

After inspecting his army Akbar said, "A fourth part has been achieved: I have seen satisfied people. The rest we shall see after a day of heat, after a day of rain, after a sleepless night."

311. Now, if you are asked, "Do you recognize astrology?" answer, "Do you deny medicine?"

If you are asked, "Do you insist upon the life of the spirit?" answer, "Do you deny the development of matter?"

If asked, "Why do you care about dead and gone Teachers?" answer, "Is it possible that science is still inaccessible to you?"

If it is said to you, "Apparently you are not averse to reading parchments," reply, "Go back to school, we will talk afterwards."

If you are asked, "How do you picture the universe?" answer, "As a drop of water."

If asked, "Why did you yourself acknowledge the Teacher?" answer, "Because He Himself has addressed us, for the development of our knowledge."

312. I shall specify the qualities distinctive in those seeking the Common Good. First—constancy of striving. Second—ability of containment, for poor is he who denies but the seeker of truth is worthy to work for General Good. Third—ability to labor, because the majority do not know the value of time. Fourth—the desire to help, without prejudices and without usurpation. Fifth—renouncement of personal property and the acceptance for safekeeping of the fruit of the creativeness of others. Sixth—expulsion of fear. Seventh—display of vigilance amidst darkness.

This must be told to those who, possessed by fear, shield themselves with denial.

One should point out that millions of people await the opening of the Gates. The shackles of hardships should not be replaced by the fetters of fear. Fear can be compared to leprosy; both cover the man with a rime of repulsiveness.

The greyish twilight of servility has brought on a wretched conception of life! Now this must end in storm and tempest.

313. No clairvoyance is equal to the spirit-knowledge. The truth can come through this knowledge. The understanding of the needs of the time comes only by this path.

Prophetic ecstasy avoids exactness of time and place, but the knowledge of the spirit foresees the quality of an event. And the way of this straight-knowledge comes into bloom without visible signs, but it is based upon the opening of the nerve centers.

The priests of old considered the spirit-knowledge to be the highest manifestation, for it could not be attained by any bodily exercises but was achieved through the accumulations of former lives.

Therefore, the care of the spirit-knowledge is expressed not in exercises but by the improvement of the life conditions of the blood vessels which feed the nerves. The principal attention must be paid to the blood pressure, because when the nerves absorb the emanations of the white blood corpuscles the opposite polarity especially reacts.

314. People will ask: "Who is greater, Christ or Buddha?" Answer: "It is impossible to measure the far-off worlds. We can only be enraptured by their radiance." The Ray of Christ feeds the Earth as much as the Rainbow of Buddha bears the affirmation of the law of life.

The New World will manifest the affirmation of fearless cognition. There the Images of the Teachers will enter into life as Friends. The Decree of the Teachers will be upon the shelf dedicated to beloved books.

In the period of the abolition of money it is urgent to replace its power by affirmation of the spirit's power to help. Knowledge must finally build scientifically the bridge of aspiration towards the spirit.

The deplorable condition of the Societies for Psychic Research must be replaced by a fearless and truthful judgment.

How can one sit together with hypocrites and liars who excellently guard their pockets!

Achievement must be made manifest and freed from the dust of prejudices.

Can a respectable man concern himself with an achievement? He has not enough room on his chest to hold all the earthly decorations. He is at a loss how to uphold all of grandfather's customs. But customs make one customary. Therefore, I urge you to look at the sky as if for the first time.

I urge you to view with horror the filth of cities as if for the first time.

I urge you to think about Christ and Buddha as if for the first time.

I urge you to look at yourself as if for the first time.

I urge you to picture the New World as if for the first time.

The least particle of personal property of bygone days is like a millstone around one's neck.

315. Unexpectedness is the sister of mobility. Mobility is the sister of achievement. Achievement is the brother of victory. For each achievement contains within itself a victory; perhaps an invisible one but one moving profound expanses.

316. What suffers most of all? Of course co-measurement! I have spoken so much about it, yet again

it is necessary to return to the old theme. Even the few who sense the importance of co-measurement remember about it only in some special circumstances. When one is drowning, then the best precepts are called to mind. Far more important is it to remember them amidst everyday life. The smallest thoughts will be borne away by the whirlwind of a right judgment. Good or bad, useful or harmful, these will be singled out, because where the big trees are, the shrubs are not seen.

If we apply our efforts to change the hustle and bustle into a beautiful achievement, then the gnarled thorn bushes will be transformed at once into a tall grove. If we can rise in thought to the boundaries of the miraculous, then we shall not speak lengthily about a worn-out sole.

I strongly advise to abolish gossip. Half the day will then be made free, and there will remain a lonely cup of coffee or glass of beer.

The time for meals must be shortened, in order to preserve the human aspect. There is no worse act of non-comeasurement than to prattle at the dinner table about trifles. There is no worse act of non-comeasurement than to toss slander like a shower of small peas. There is no worse act of non-comeasurement than to defer an urgent action. There is no worse act of non-comeasurement than to show offense like a petty huckster. There is no worse act of non-comeasurement than to renounce responsibility. There is no worse act of non-comeasurement than to cease thinking about beauty. Co-measurement is like the pillar that supports the house.

When we take into consideration the painting of the dwelling, are we to destroy the pillar under the archway? Thoroughly assimilate co-measurement.

317. If co-measurement is not observed, then the determination is also destroyed. Our determination is up to the last limit. It is not that determination which proceeds in comfort and fits in with personal habits. Not that determination which is to the body's advantage. Our determination is confined only by the spirit's limits. Therefore, it is impossible to bar the way of Our Striving. Warriors and builders of life proceed with Our determination.

If timidity retards one, then it is better to burn the bridges already crossed. If avarice hinders, then better throw the purse over the next river. If stupidity impedes, then better let one's horses go by themselves. If rancour delays, then better hang an effigy of the enemy between the ears of one's horse. Only beauty can promote determination. Then to think about the purse and the enemy will seem a child's whim.

As the center of a magnet attracts toward itself, so the fundamental quality of resoluteness is invincible. Indeed, the invincibility of determination is convincing, and it is an immutable condition of the true mysteries. A true mystery must be regarded as a guiding action of life. Thus, Our determination is connected with the leading concept. Put determination into practice.

318. Determination conditions the law of occult facets. Even a stone is cut in facets for the manifestation of the inner fire. Likewise, the path to the Light is divided by clearly discernible lines. Of course, instead of facets one can always make heaps of broken stones, but this is deplorable.

A rational path is divided into periods of about a thousand days each. The three years of these periods, similar in exterior aspect, completely differ as to the qualities of spiritual consciousness concerned.

The sharper the line of distinction, the more conformable to the plan is the path. Usually the first year of the three-year period is characterized as preparatory, the second is an active one, the third a dim and wearisome threshold.

Let us begin a new period. It may be called "earthly homelessness." One must cast aside all past considerations and rush into a desert of boundless stillness, where thunderstorms and whirlwinds entwine one under a radiant dome. Amidst the storms a new raiment will be woven.

Let the next period be called "The Luminous," and thus let us build it. Let us courageously turn the steeds into the haze of the desert. The experience of homeless wandering must be lived through. In like manner have walked all Seekers.

One can welcome this period, when the boundaries between countries are being erased.

319. About occult murder.

Invisible slayings are incomparably more numerous than the bloody ones. Out of hatred, out of ignorance, out of fear, men implant poisoned arrows, the force of which is great. One of the best means of defense is the concept of an occult circle. But the best remedy must be taken according to exact indications.

The power of the circle is so great that even stellar decrees can be modified. It is known that the circle has shifted sickness and death.

Because of its significance, the circle must be guarded, like any tuned instrument. One should not forget that every action between members of the circle must be circumspect. Everything useful can be turned into an injury, if there be tolerated the throwing of stones into the brother's orchard. And can one know where a foolishly thrown stone will strike? Often the condition of auras deflects the stone and, instead of a foot, it strikes the temple.

Therefore, it is indispensable to put the stones out of action and with all strength to guard the treasure of the circle. I have forewarned.

320. About the qualities of action.

If an action is small, it needs the help of various handmade objects. But when the action becomes great it can dispense with earthly objects. This is the first touchstone of action.

When the magician speaks about a whole pharmacy, it means his action is one of very small dimension.

The second quality of action is its mobility. Like a whirlwind of primary matter, a true action must vibrate with possibilities. Only a flight can crown a luminous manifested thought.

The third quality of action is its unexpected-ness. Every action which has astounded the minds of the people was the result of an unexpected way of thinking.

The fourth quality of action is its elusiveness. Only this quality protects the action against destructive attacks.

The fifth quality of action is its convincingness. As every lightning flash connects our consciousness with the Cosmos, so each action should strike like a flashing sword.

The sixth quality of action is its lawfulness. Only the consciousness of the fundamentals of the world evolution will advance the action immutably.

The seventh quality of action is its pure motive. By this path one can move weighty loads without fatigue.

One must equally well comprehend the actions of the body and those of spirit. Because, after all that has been said, the action of thought is still not appreciated.

I wish to speak particularly to those who place their trust in matter: Your thought is imbued with the emanations of nerve centers, and according to its specific gravity it is heavier than many microorganisms. Is then your thought not matter? How exactly must we, then, weigh our thoughts! We are responsible for them, just as a man who misuses charcoal fumes is responsible.

It is simpler to think beginning with matter. For where are its limits? Thus, the teaching of the spirit will stand alongside that of matter. So they who deny the spirit will also be denying matter.

321. About the qualities of expectancy.

The highest expectancy is that of the evolution of the world. The usual expectations are divided into the dark, the sluggish, and the vigilant. The chaos of the dark ones brings only harm to space. The sluggish expectations are like smouldering coals.

The vigilant expectations manifest readiness to accept the new at every hour.

I have said, "Know how to desire." I will also say, "Know how to await." Be able to purify the quality of expectation. Through storm carry expectation as an inextinguishable torch.

The inner quality of expectancy is its growth in tensity. With what could one best correlate this sign, if not with the evolution of the World? Such expectancy should penetrate your whole life and fill your work with the throbbing of action. For in this union is the best and most beautiful.

Upon entering a house full of restless people, say to them: "Look forward to the evolution of the world!"

322. It will be asked: "How can you refer to a Creator Whom you do not know?"

Reply: "Historically and scientifically we know the Great Teachers who have created the quality of our consciousness."

152

"In recognizing the influence of the ideology of the Teachers, are you not restricting your freedom?"

Reply: "The quality of freedom is remarkable; if freedom exists at all, nothing can limit it. The body can be shackled, but nothing can diminish consciousness except ugliness. When we touch upon the heights of freedom, we must guard against ugliness. If we wish to exalt matter, we must think wisely about beauty."

In Beauty will Infinity be manifested. In Beauty the teachings of the Seekers of the spirit are illumined. In Beauty we do not fear to manifest the truth of freedom. In Beauty do we kindle radiance in every drop of water. In Beauty do we transform matter into a rainbow.

There is no ugliness which will not be engulfed in the rays of the rainbow. There are no fetters which will not disintegrate in the freedom of Beauty.

How shall we find the words to approach the concept of the universe? How shall we tell about the evolution of forms? How to uplift the consciousness to the study of fundamentals? How to stimulate humanity to scientific cognition of the worlds?

Each realization is born in Beauty.

Know how to think radiantly, and nothing terrifying will touch you. Remember, We have no forbiddances.

323. It has been said that he who speaks against the spirit shows himself ignorant, and that blasphemy against the Spirit is the worst of all.

Saints have been spoken about, but to whom can this inexplicable concept be applied?

Those who perform miracles will be learned magicians. Those who keep their lives in purity will be practical people. Only those who have consciously renounced all the personal and who have transported their consciousness into the conception of world evolution can be called saints in Our understanding.

It is imperative that this process be accomplished consciously, outside of fortuitous external conditions.

It is impossible to forcibly implant religion anew—it would be but a sacrilegious monstrosity.

The way of renouncing the ugliness of life will prompt the spirit to truthful quests. Then the obviousness of the interrelation of the worlds will compel one to ponder scientifically.

This ineffable thought is the beginning of spiritual discipline. These quests, void of the personal element, awaken the reflex of action—this is called achievement.

It is better, in general, to replace the word "saint" with an absolutely definite term—achiever. The manifestation of achievement in life is unceasing, and without hypocrisy We will be able thus to proclaim its evident manifestations.

Life's achievement must be performed by human hands.

324. A prophet is a man who possesses spiritual foresight. Just as on the physical plane there is nearsightedness and farsightedness, thus simply must one understand the quality of farsightedness of the spirit.

It would be absolutely the height of ignorance to deny all prophecies.

It would be completely stupid to condemn the prophets.

If we scientifically and impartially examine prophecies which have chanced to be preserved, what do we see? We find people who, disregarding personal advantage or disadvantage, have peered into a forthcoming page of history, were terrified, and forewarned the people.

Among known prophecies one does not find selfish intentions, one does not find a criminal self-interest, one does not find slander. The symbols of visions are tinted because of the distance, and difference in space and time.

When will scholars find time to investigate prophecies scientifically and to make historical comparisons?

It would be a fine book for a young scientist to write!

Yes, friends, it is time to learn to approach obvious manifestations culturally. Otherwise, future attainments will be to men what electrons are to cradled infants. Your uniforms and togas do not conceal your timorous infancy.

You will ask who determined your rankings and denominations. Verily, you would be horrified to see the forefathers of your contentment. Dwarfs of cupidity attempted to screen the Giants of the Common Weal.

The radiance of the New World does not penetrate into your burrow! But let a whirlwind sweep away the roots which shroud the Dawn!

325. Can it be so very difficult for you to understand the meaning of astrology? If knowledge of it is lacking, I suggest making an experiment. Suppose you take four organisms: a plant, a fish, a bird, and an animal—let us say a lily, a carp, a dove, and a dog. Provide seven specimens of each, and for each group construct a place deprived of daylight and saturated with a colored electric light. The glass should be of various colors, conforming as closely as possible to the colors of the rainbow. At night you should merely reduce the amount of light. Thus you may observe them for about four months.

At the end of this time even a blind man will grasp the difference in the results. Besides, there will be lacking the principle factor of the stellar ray; namely, its chemical composition. It is impossible to ignore the importance of the physical influence of the planetary bodies.

The attention and expectations of humanity must be turned to the far-off worlds. Hence, everything pertaining to this subject must be studied without prejudices. Since exact knowledge is needed, astronomy is strikingly applicable.

326. It is possible to issue decrees, to make promises, and to intimidate; but only understanding impels. What could replace the understanding of applicability?

People will say, "How beautiful! How powerful! How sublime!" But all these outbursts are like will-o-the-wisps over a marsh, and are extinguished as easily as they are generated. Pure but superficial thoughts are like multi-colored dust particles; the first wind carries them away into space. The value of such particles is negligible.

We appreciate a thought which has engendered a decision. The decision is valued according to its applicability. Applicability is judged by spirit-knowledge, and then an action results at which one may rejoice. Whoever rejoices has faith also. Even faith must be well-grounded, and thus can the Teaching live.

We compute well, We apply well. If you are accused of economy, do not reject this either; for economy is opposed to madness, and madness is opposed to spirit-knowledge. But whatever circle of reasoning we choose, we shall inevitably return to the great knowledge of the spirit.

I do not vaguely feel, I know! Not superstition, but certainty. When we are filled with immutability, it is as if we have contacted the magnet of the planet. Then we stand steadfast.

327. Avoid uniformity, as to both place and work. Actually, uniformity accompanies that greatest fallacy, the concept of personal ownership. First of all, the slave of property loses mobility of spirit. Such a slave

ceases to understand that each day of labor should be tinged with a special quality of the spirit. He cannot change place, because his spirit will be permanently fixed in his earthly home.

Ask yourself—is it easy for you to move to another place? Is it easy for you to change the nature of your work? If it is, this means that you can appreciate the value of the Common Good.

If each journey forces you to write your last will and testament, and a change of work makes you unhappy, this means that a remedy must be taken. Most dangerous journeys should be prescribed, and changes in the way of most diversified work should be assigned. This will develop courage and resourcefulness, because the primary cause of the defect is fear.

The embryo of proprietorship is also fear, the feeling that one must be attached to the Earth at least by something! As if a miserable hovel could be an adequate anchor for the spirit! As if a heap of personal belongings could protect one from the lightning! Periodically the injurious playthings of ownership have been taken away from humanity. But again fear, the father of lies, spins his cobweb and again terrors are concocted. Therefore, let us abolish fear. With it will depart property ownership and boredom.

How much new health there is in diversity of place and of labor!

328. Nirvana is the quality of assimilation of all actions. The saturation of all-inclusiveness brings you true knowledge, flowing from the tremor of illumination. Languages have no more precise definition of this process. Quietude is only an external aspect, and quietude does not express the essential nature of the condition.

Buddha mentioned quietude, but only this external

aspect was assimilated by his listeners. For to the people who heard him the idea of rest was very attractive. Action as something meritorious is too little understood.

You like scientific construction—so do We. If you have heard the theory of vortical rings, the theory of waves, of magnetism, of attraction and repulsion, then you must realize that there exist on the Earth places of very diverse significance. Even dull-witted heads have pondered over the strange fate of many cities. The combination of a physicist, an astrochemist, a biologist, and an astrologer would yield the best answer without any mysticism. The construction of large cities ought to be cautiously planned. Least significant of all is contemporary politics, because this concept lacks scientific basis and beauty.

Gauging the requirements of the future city, be not misled by an apparently broad concept; a trifle is often more indicative.

Also, in selecting coworkers pay attention to details during small actions.

Determining the essential nature of a man through the pupil of his eye, We surround him with habits of small actions. Least of all attach significance to words; they are as flowing waters. Small actions which saturate the whole life best denote the nature of a man—from them grow the large ones. We do not place much trust in chance achievements. From fear one can accomplish a deed of courage.

Conscious actions are necessary; they alone lead to Nirvana.

329. Let us imagine a man imbued with the thought that his two eyes see differently. Of course he will be right, but by this very thought he will ruin his eyesight. Coordination of reflexes is difficult, but it alone

assures successful operation of the apparatus. The difference between the eyes is what gives perspective to the thing seen.

Just so can two different truths coalesce in a healthy organism. A man who is obsessed with thought about different truths is like the man who ponders about the difference of his eyes, he loses perspective of conception.

330. Outside the window sounded a call. One worker ignored it with "Don't disturb me, I am busy!" Another promised to come but forgot. A third came after his work was finished, but the place was already empty. A fourth was set atremble at the call, and, putting aside his tools, went forth at once with, "Here I am!" This is called the tremor of sensitiveness.

Only this tremor, lit by the consciousness day and night, leads to spirit-knowledge. Over and above the reason, the gates are opened by a tremor which is even audible to human apparati.

If you are unable to suppress within yourself this tremor of sensitiveness—good for you!

331. Ask a composer if he likes unison choirs and symphonies. He will pronounce your question an absurdity, because there is no such thing as a symphony in unison. For a new tone the composer is ready to introduce the most unexpected instrument. Just so in the formation of a group—be not astonished at an apparent diversity of the members. Not according to birth, nor habits, nor mistakes are they grouped; their contact is in spirit. They are united in a chorus by spirit, which is imponderable, invisible and inaudible. Therefore, do not reproach anyone for the pitch of his voice—its quality is what is important.

It is joyous to realize that quality can always be improved if there is discipline of spirit.

332. In creeds and laws treachery, slander, and revilement are condemned; but it is not adequately shown why these actions are essentially harmful. Hence, these censures have the appearance of prohibitions. But any forbiddance is relative and unconvincing. When harm and usefulness are indicated, the essential nature must be explained.

The harm of treachery, slander and revilement can easily be shown in an ordinary example. Of course, the ultimate injury will be not to the betrayed but to the betrayer.

The entire world is divided along a boundary line between individual and general welfare. If we act within the sphere of the general welfare with sincere intentions, then in support of us stands the entire reservoir of cosmic accumulations. This chalice of the best achievements begins to act along an invisible ray.

Imagine it this way: A candle filled with malice is trying to burn you. You have not yet taken any measures, but from behind you there is approaching a powerful torch. Perform this experiment and you will see how the candle gutters, chars, and goes out.

It is not a punishment but a consequence of the laws of nature.

People betray, slander, and revile the bearers of the Common Weal, but not enviable is the fate of these carriers of singeing fires. Therefore, treachery, slander and revilement are not practical.

Therefore, think not about revenge; for even the ancients effectively said,

" 'Vengeance is mine,' saith the Lord." Is the life of a traitor an easy one?

Likewise, in creeds and laws theft has been spoken against, but again this sounds like a prohibition. Whereas, it must be pointed out that theft is harmful as a concept which augments the sense of personal ownership. Theft injures world evolution, and not enviable is the lot of those who harm world evolution. They send themselves a long way backward.

It is unimportant that some object passes into other hands, but what is important is that two men will experience the onset of the sense of personal ownership.

The law concerning theft is incomplete, because the principal thefts are those of knowledge and creative ideas, which cannot be guarded against.

Theft will be abolished with the elimination of privately owned property.

333. In creeds and laws intemperance is much condemned, but again without explanation. The practicality of temperateness in food and speech can be seen over a period of several months. Of course, as always, We are opposed to fanaticism and torments; the body knows it full needs. About sexual temperance it is necessary to speak in more detail; too much space has been allotted this subject by contemporary thinking.

Very ancient mysteries said: "The lingam is the vessel of wisdom," but in time this knowledge was converted into hideous phallic cults, and religion began to prohibit something without knowing exactly why. Whereas, it should have been said simply that the fact of conception is so wondrous that it is impossible to deal with it by ordinary measures.

One may weigh, one may analyze up to the most minute particles, but still there remains an imperceptible and inscrutable substance, as irreplaceable as the vital force of a seed. In due time We shall direct attention to certain striking properties of this substance, which can be seen; but now it must be agreed that such an extraordinary substance must be very precious and must have some extremely important qualities—even a fool will comprehend this. Experiment provides certainly the best proof. If we compare two individuals, of whom one dissipates the vital substance while the other consciously conserves it, we will be amazed at how much more sensitive the spiritual apparatus of the second becomes. The quality of his labors becomes entirely different, and the quantity of his projects and ideas multiplies. The centers of the solar plexus and brain are being heated, as it were, by an invisible fire. That is why temperance is not a pathological renunciation but a sensible action. To bestow life does not mean to cast away the entire supply of vital substance.

If at the first step people would at least remember the value of the vital substance, then by this alone the necessity of prohibitions would be notably reduced. Forbiddance must be done away with; this is a law of striving. But an irreplaceable treasure will be preserved, and this also is a law of striving.

Let us look at things more veraciously—everything irreplaceable will be in the prime places of conservation.

Can we actually cast the treasure away into space? Indeed, this energy will adhere to the elements from which it has been extracted with such difficulty; and instead of cooperation with evolution there results rubbish, which is subject to a reworking.

Thus, let us picture temperance as wings!

334. Two signs of the authenticity of the Teaching are: first, striving for the Common Weal; second, acceptance of all previous Teachings which are congruous with the first sign. It must be noted that the primary form of a Teaching does not contain negative postulates. But superstitious followers begin to fence in the Covenants with negations, obstructing the good. There results the ruinous formula: "Our creed is the

best," or, "We are the true believers; all others are infidels." From this point it is a single step to the Crusades, to the Inquisition, and to seas of blood in the name of Those Who condemned killing. There is no worse occupation than forcible imposition of one's creed.

Whoever wishes to follow Us must first of all forget negation and freely bear the renewed life without constraint of others. People are attracted by beauty and by luminous knowledge. Only that Teaching which contains all hope, which makes life beautiful, which manifests action, can promote true evolution. Certainly life is not a market, where one can make a fine bargain for entrance into the Heavenly Kingdom. Certainly life is not a grave, where one trembles before the justice of an Unknown Judge!

In keeping with their opinion, scholars have proposed the ingenious consolation: "Man begins to die from the moment of his birth"—a scanty and funereal comfort. But We say that man is eternally being born, and particularly at the moment of so-called death.

The servitors of distorted religions encourage their wards in the purchase of places in the cemetery, where through their advance arrangements they will lie more advantageously and honorably than others more indigent and hence undeserving of lengthy prayers. The incense for these poor ones will be adulterated and the prayers abominably sung.

Ask people, finally, what authentic Teaching has enjoined this monstrous practice? Verily, we have had enough of graves, cemeteries, and intimidations!

One may know how loftily the Teachers have regarded the transition to future manifestations, and least of all have They been concerned about a cemetery site.

The attitude toward death is a very important

indicator of the character of the Teaching, for in it is contained the understanding of reincarnation.

I urge you to consider reincarnation strictly scientifically.

If you can propound any other structure of the universe, We shall reserve for you a chair as professor of theology and promise you a first-class funeral; for indeed in the eyes of the enlightened you will have already decided to die.

Read attentively the writings of the Teachers published by you, and you will be amazed at how unanimously in all ages They speak about the change of life.

The Path of Light will appear when you venture to look scientifically and without prejudices.

The daring ones are with Us—joy to the daring ones!

335. Action of the spirit is incalculably swift. Thought is a reflex of the spirit; hence the motion of thought is incredibly rapid.

Only after many steps on a slow scale is the calculation of the speed of light begun.

Since the significance of the spirit is great, then great value should be attached to thought, the child of the spirit. What significance thought has is shown even by a simple apparatus for study of the spectrum of the aura. The aura changes color not only from realized thoughts but, in the same measure, from the errant flies of our spirit reservoir which do not reach the reason nor the memory.

The identical significance of thought and action is spoken about everywhere. This is easily established. Note the effects of a thought about murder and of the act of murder upon the spectrum of the aura—the results will be identical. It is difficult for people to assimilate the fact that the thought has the same effect as the deed. But whoever wishes to take part in world evolution must understand the significance of thought. When thoughts are transformed into physical colors, their action at a distance is just as evident as that revealed by the study of light waves. One must approach scientifically the theory of the force of thought. One should not refer this to exceptional personalities-this law is common to all. Its principal effect will be recognition of the impracticality of falsehood and hypocrisy as well as the need of solicitude toward one's near ones.

Open minded scholars know that by a single fleeting thought the entire aura is physically colored. The thought may seem to be absolutely secret, yet it has in effect a physical color, scientifically ascertained.

A measuring scale for auras will provide adequate proof for the ignorant.

We have to deal with civilized ignoramuses as with children. A burnt finger teaches them the proper handling of fire. We speak about prejudices, but every state official does not know what a savage beast prejudice is. Let us proceed to joy!

336. Some say that work can be fatiguing and even injurious to the health. Thus say lazy and inert people.

Understand that work properly apportioned cannot in itself be fatiguing. One should understand how to effect a proper change of the group of working nerves, and then no fatigue can find access. Do not try to find rest in idleness. Idleness is but the microbe of indolence. Muscles may ache after tension, but you have but to plunge into idleness to begin to feel the full pain. Whereas, by calling into action the opposite centers one can completely avoid the reflex of the previous tension. Indeed, implicit herein is a great mobility, which is developed by conscious experience.

When a physician prescribes a diversified treatment,

time and opportunities are found to carry it out. In the same way one can find a rational change of work. This concerns all kinds of labor.

It is sad to come upon that immobility of mind which impedes the work of the higher centers.

It must be kept in mind that certain bodily positions should be avoided—or at least often changed. Stooping from a standing position interferes with the solar plexus. Throwing the head back hampers the brain centers. Arms stretched forward overburden the center of the aorta. Lying on the back may impede the center of kundalini, though it also may stimulate it. Clear thinking may come with a rush when the position of the light is improved. One has but to turn oneself toward the light or away from it and the reaction is perceptible. First of all, remember that each position has its advantage, but if one is turned into a weather-vane for every shifting wind, then the system of ascent will be disrupted.

337. Success will not abandon those who are striving impetuously, for it is difficult to strike an arrow in flight. How swiftly approaching are the dates of those predestined ones, yet in movement yesterday must be distinguished from tomorrow.

Nations have rebelled, kings are departing—is this by chance? Only the blind do not perceive the movement of evolution. Every youthful heart quivers with a presentiment of new forms. In these movements each new form, though imperfect, is more valuable than the polished old one.

If one is to call oneself a sun-bearer, one must forget about darkness.

Can one aught but uphold those who are striving toward the sun? It is easier to explain to them the significance of the solar prana. The solar ray will illumine for them new depths—but one must accept.

Each summoned one is offered the entire chalice. If he does not receive the messenger, he will get only a portion of what has been decreed. If he cannot assimilate this part, he will be given a still smaller particle—thus does each one determine his own allotment.

It must be said to those choosing a lesser portion: "Self-belittlers, you have driven yourselves from the garden through habits of lightmindedness! Perceive how easy it would have been to acknowledge the messenger of the chalice. Together with him you could have planted a seedling of great freedom. How hard it is now to look into the eyes of passers-by, seeking him who sought admittance to you. What is easy today is inaccessible tomorrow. Therefore, gird yourselves with all vigilance."

One can repeat a Decree, but it is impossible to open eyes forcibly. Let the sleeper continue his slumber! But could one sleep through a time of scintillation of the sky and trembling of the whole earth?

338. Let us recall several cases of error repeated many times in different lives. People have awaited the Messenger for ten years yet closed the door on the day before His coming. Choosing the least portion, they have imagined that all was permitted and tolerated. Selecting a particle, they have fallen into blissful inaction and wondered why the particle wasted away. Choosing a particle, they have decided to retain old habits—as if on one side of the bosom could repose the portion of good and on the other could be kept pet cockroaches. Choosing a particle, they have decided to jump off the train for only a minute, forgetting that such a leap in motion carries one perilously backward. Choosing a particle, they have thought to slander a brother, forgetting that the slander would beat back painfully on their own foreheads.

You may ask: "How should one conduct oneself so as not to besmirch the chosen portion?" I can give this advice: Instead of a particle, accept the entire chalice of the Common Good. This will shield you against all impurities. Instead of timorous hesitation, resolve as an experiment to adopt for seven years the plan of the General Welfare. If My advice is poor, you can return later to breeding your cockroaches.

To whomever the Chalice of the Common Good seems heavy, I shall say that the Teaching is not sugar-coated nuts and it is not silver trinkets. The Teaching is rich silver ore, destined and treasured. The Teaching is curative resin, revealed and directed.

I shall tell the wavering one that he must beware of becoming a traitor, because the fate of even a small traitor is horrible!

I shall say to the toiler that to attract a small force is of considerable merit, but to attract a great force is a luminous achievement. Verily, the chalice of the Common Weal is not weighty to the toiler.

When you are seeking coworkers, do not be confused. Working hands may disguise the Messenger; His complexion may be due to the mountain snows. The Messenger of Truth will not be shouting in the bazaar.

Thus gather the signs—the time is near!

339. Now that you have assimilated the distinguishing marks of the Messenger, We shall remind you of the characteristics of coworkers. They are without prejudices, mobile in action, young in spirit, fearless of chasms. It is well not to forget the unknown ones and the orphans.

Now it is time to speak of the signs of the path leading to Us. First of all, do you clearly accept the existence of the Teachers?

When you read about a discovery of dinosaur eggs,

you readily accept the information. Just as easily do you accept information about a new species of ape; about the vital capacity of seeds found in the tombs of the Pyramids; about an unknown metal; about a new tribe of descendants of island castaways. A whole train of information outside of your everyday life you accept without demur.

Is it difficult to accept the fact that a group that has acquired knowledge by the path of tenacious labor can be united in the name of the Common Good? Empirical knowledge has led to the finding of a favorable place, where the currents permit easier communications in diverse directions.

Surely you have heard the accounts of travelers about discovering unknown Yogis in caves. If you extend this fact in the direction of actual knowledge, you will easily arrive at the perception of the group of Teachers of Knowledge.

How then to find the way to Our Laboratories? Without a summons, no one will reach Us. Without a Guide no one will pass! At the same time there is necessary an indomitable personal striving and readiness for the hardships of the way.

According to custom the wayfarer must traverse a certain portion of the way alone. Just before arrival, even those who have been in direct communication with Us do not sense Our tidings. It must be thus because of human conditions.

Those arriving alone, except for profound reasons, are divided into two groups: those striving personally and those summoned for a mission.

Without a special Indication, no one will recognize those who have been to see Us.

Since Our Messenger does not shout in the market

place, so too those who have been with Us know how to guard the Common Weal.

An unmistakable sign of Our Call is when you are borne irresistibly, as if on wings. Thus accept Our Community of Knowledge and Beauty. And be assured that, although one can search every mountain gorge, an uninvited visitor will not find the way.

Many times have We visited your cities, and no one can say We are estranged from the world. You yourselves locate your observatories outside cities, and take care to leave scientists in quietude. Accept, then, Our considerations, and be not vexed at the lack of a definite address.

Remember Those working for the Common Good!

340. You will inevitably encounter a certain kind of people who fly into a rage at mention of the Teachers. They are ready to trust in any despicable stock market speculation, they are ready to believe in any swindle, but the idea of the General Welfare is inadmissible to them.

Look intently into the pupil of the eye of these people. Therein you will find an evasive shadow, and they cannot long endure your gaze. These are hidden dugpas. Often they are more dangerous than their more obvious colleagues.

Even if a purse of money is sent to them, they will recall a non-existent debtor. If they are saved from ruin, their gratitude will go to the police. Even if one should bring these seemingly well-intentioned people to the very boundary of Our Abode they will declare that what is seen is a mirage. It might be thought that this is due to ignorance, but the reason is far worse.

Beware of them! Chiefly, protect the children. They are the cause of many children's ailments. They find access into the schools. For them historical fact and the law of knowledge are non-existent. Upon encountering sickly children inquire about the quality of their teachers.

Just now, when an important time is drawing near, it is necessary to disinfect as many children as possible; they will be the ones to think about the cities of the future. They must be given a truthful book about the saintly heroes of the Common Good, but this book has not yet been written. Fallacious are children's books, spurious their playthings, false the smiles of their tutors. Amidst constant falsification is it possible to expect truthfulness?

I advise to devote time to the children. Let them carry stones and timbers for their city.

I have spoken about secret dugpas for your information; but for yourselves you need pay no attention to them, as to every striving worker they are mere dust.

But if you show children Our Domicile, they will joyously walk through all the laboratories and observatories. Our prismatic mirrors will give them unforgettable joy; because they love everything real, and We Ourselves strive for Truth.

Give the children only real, true objects!

341. From Our Community We sow seeds of the Common Good throughout all parts of the world. You ask how to keep the Code of the Community? You have already heard about many features of Our Labor, and now remember this not merely for information but for immediate application. If renouncement of the personal brings one near, then abstinence from action for the Common Good removes one immeasurably—this is a rule of the Community. Through mobility of mind it is easy to preserve the personal during striving for the General Welfare.

You ask why so many tests are necessary. In the

Community everything is attained by experience; therefore, it is right to regard testings as growth. Tests lie as thresholds to the gates of Beauty.

Do away with sighing and tearful faces when speaking about tests.

Rejection of the Common Good casts even a giant into a pit.

Whoever has had the advantage of listening to Our discourses can testify as to how efficiently and amidst what diverse activities Our time passes. For the increase of possibilities, We have been obliged to curtail lengthy forms of speech, seeking in different ages the better and briefer definitives. It is necessary to be able to give in three minutes' time the salient contents of a three-hour speech. In saying this, I am ignoring the indignation of lawyers and preachers.

To evaluate the treasure of time is possible only through labor for the General Welfare. Least of all is it admissible to steal the time of one's brother. Aimlessly stealing time is the same as stealing ideas.

To the testing there may be added a question that even a child can be asked: "What do you consider of the utmost importance right now?" Understanding the train of thought, one can recognize the true nature according to the reply. It is sad to look upon those who conceal their thoughts. Thought is lightning.

342. He who has dedicated himself to a hencoop receives results in eggs. He who has dedicated himself to a part of the world vibrates with the soil.

People have distorted the meaning of the word "harmony." Into this concept there has been inserted something clerical, a fold of the chiton, the immortelle of non-existent love, and even a knitted stocking. It were better, without any harps, to replace this withered concept with a more energetic one: let us say "sensitiveness of cooperation." Without it the Community cannot exist. Violation of it provokes resentment; resentment begets dullness and stupidity.

A man who is depressed by resentment is attracted to a single point. Becoming immobile, the man inevitably becomes dull. Dullness, like rust, corrodes a portion of the fundamental substance.

Everything vibrates, undulates, and breathes amidst lightning flashes.

In the days of great constructions do not tolerate a rusty anchor; rust will not withstand a sweeping vortex!

343. A physician may ask: "If the aura is a physical manifestation, then can it not be grown from without, physically?" To a certain extent this will be right.

We have already heard about external blows striking upon the aura. Likewise, there can be created a hothouse atmosphere which heals the aura, but hothouse conditions are the same everywhere and they are not suitable for evolution.

Just as the organism must be developed from within, independent of external conditions, so too the firmness and the purport of the aura grow only from within. Straightened conditions are especially useful for breadth of the aura. The generosity of the hand does not depend upon the quantity it gives.

I see a young scientist who has collected covenants from all the Teachings of the East and who says to himself, "From all sides I shall select the precepts of life; I shall discard all hymns and ritualistic worship; I shall disregard the difference in time and the errors of slanderers and translators, as the very simplest appears to be the most fundamental. From these fragments I shall compose here a single life—this is the life of the East. Notwithstanding its

173

fragmentariness, this life will be wise and full of evolutionary actions."

Why have all Teachings been engendered in Asia? What magnets have collected there the progressive energy of the spirit?

For a waterspout there is needed joint action from above and below. And does not the utmost antiquity respond to the wings of the future?

The antiquity of Atlantis can respond to flight beyond the planet. So broad are these gates that all the rest enters easily!

344. Can Our Community intervene in the affairs of the world and render active assistance?

Every community is devoid of egotism, in its vulgar meaning, and in the name of the Common Good is concerned with the solution of world affairs. Like arrows plunge the sendings of the Community into the brains of humanity.

There can be traced in scientific literature a series of psychic and physical effects. There are well-known cases of the sending of objects of great significance. There are known dispatches of sums of money. There are known forewarnings of danger. There are known letters about the solution of affairs. There are known meetings under various aspects. We have had steamship tickets and costumes of different countries. We have had different names and have appeared when circumstances imperatively required it.

Already I see that someone is indignant and calls the above "fairy tales." Whereas, before his eyes a university received a donation from an unknown person, and also to an acquaintance of his there was brought a valuable bust from someone unknown.

Our envoy once urged a queen to act more in accord with the laws of the time. Our envoy has counseled a young inventor. Our envoy guided a promising scholar. A list can be shown of persons who have received monetary sendings. These are all facts, attested by physical documents.

Why does this seem mystical and mysterious to some, when everyone has done the same thing in a lesser measure?

Once the principle of the Common Good has been inculcated in humanity, then by carrying it further we secure a Community strong through experience.

Only the blind do not notice whither the spiral of evolution has turned! And We, Who do exist, send help to the young in spirit.

345. Since Our Central Community does have significance for world structures, then, too, communities established by Us have an influence upon the evolution of the world. Let us examine the principal kinds of these widely scattered communities.

The first are the unconscious communities whose members work out a mutually acceptable way of co-existence. These can be found among workmen, farmers, students, and, less frequently, in families.

The second kind of community knows about the plan of earthly evolution, but does not connect this plan with definite action and date. These are circles of political idealists; certain occult organizations; some learned societies; and—rarest of all—clerical bodies.

The third kind of community knows not only the plan of evolution but also the dates and the action. Of course these communities are rare, and they receive Our Indications.

He who has come in close touch with Us learns silence. Likewise, it is difficult to distinguish the participants of a community of the third kind. More talkative is the second kind of community; already they speak much about the Common Good.

Verily, the dark age will terminate with the proclaiming of the Community! Sergius hewed it out with his axe. Boehme worked on it with his boot hammer. The Teacher Buddha built it with His hands. Christ prepared a bridge to it. A most ancient Teacher said: "I do not see any objects that I own!"

Now it but remains to send upon Us a punitive expedition; but it will get nowhere, because We possess certain scientific resources.

About gases, though the subject has not yet entered this book, I have already named several powerful compounds. Beautiful and non-recurrent is the time of change after a long and grievous age!

346. An instructive case can be narrated of how unexpectedly a useful coworker reached Our Community.

You already know that before final enlistment with Us there occur particular attacks of physical weakness. This is explained by the undulatory condition of the nerve centers; there may be fainting, spasms, anguish, and aches of the different centers.

One of Our Friends once went forth by the mountain path, and, being accustomed to long marches, went beyond the protected boundary and there fell into a deep faint. What then did Our telescopic apparati show? Our Friend was lying on the brink of a very dangerous precipice. A member of a geographical expedition, having become lost from his caravan, hastened to Him. Although himself hungry and weakened, he lifted up Our Friend, Who was very tall of stature, and carried Him along the footpath. It should be explained that only by increased nerve tension could he have been able to lift such a weight. When those sent by Us arrived, the traveler himself fell into a still deeper swoon. But his excessive burden had made him Our coworker.

At present he heads the guarding of the paths and is engaged in historical researches. He often repeats: "Never fear an excessive load." Indeed, there was a reason that he should find himself in Our mountains.

The manifestation of enemies must be interpreted in connection with a certain sickly condition about which I have made mention.

Humanly it is easy to understand how disagreeable Our Community is to some. One does not have to be a wizard to imagine how some are attempting to bar the path. But these enemies are not yours nor Ours; they are enemies of enlightenment, inevitable and persistent. Therefore, We advise you to take things as they are and not to be afraid of excessive burden.

347. In the formation of new communities, it is necessary to have in mind a troublesome specific human trait—I am speaking of envy. From rivalry there gradually arises the viper of envy, and in the same nest are falsehood and hypocrisy.

The viper is small in size, and its birth is sometimes impossible to notice. Therefore, at the formation of a community it is necessary to foresee the differences between its members and to show why they cannot be duplicated nor compared, like the limbs of the body.

The time is at hand when My Teaching will not easily reach communities in different countries.

Before the issuance of the third book, one has not only to assimilate the second but also to put it into practice in life.

I already know how superficially the first book was read by many. Some made of it a dream book and fortune teller. Others took it for a soothing drug.

But few are those who took it as an urgent call to world evolution.

In the second book those who understood the summons of the first will find the features of the desired labor.

The emergence of world events will place the book on the worktable. At this table We can meet together with you. Sometimes an excessive burden becomes a feather of a wing.

348. In communal occupations, do not indulge in thoughts about the recent past; think either about the future or the wisdom of the ages. The fragments and dust of the husks of the past fill space too much. Attracted by the magnet of thought, they weave unclean phantoms which are difficult to drive away. Expelled from one corner, they camp in another, until they are again reduced to dust by a conscious stroke of the will.

It is more practical to think about the future— these thoughts have recourse to solar prana. The magnet of such thoughts can attract particles of cosmic dust. This dust of the far-off worlds is beneficial for new formations.

If astronomy equals geography, then cosmic dust equals history; and each aerolite is an archaeological object.

The historical account about Solomon revering a particular Aerolite has a scientific basis. Thus, often a fairy tale becomes a page of a scientific work.

Galileo too, in his time, related dangerous tales. Can you possibly wish to resemble the cardinals who opposed Galileo?

One must accustom oneself to thinking about the future. When you come together you must send out thoughts about the future. The assemblies will be purer.

349. Some more counsels.

To hurry and to arrive late are equally wrong; but if one has to choose between the two, then it is better to hasten. Just as it is better to omit than to add.

If complaint appears in a community, then the community is turning into a police station.

If self-love appears in a community, then the community is turning into a zoological garden.

If My Teaching is not applied in a community, it means there is someone who is masking himself.

Each one who has entered may depart, but he who leaves takes with him his acquired and real possessions.

If sometimes an excessive load is light as a feather, then often an ounce of falsehood is heavier than two score pounds.

If there appears a vehement comparison of self-merit between members of the community, this leads to a horrible manifestation of defeat.

Grievous is the path for those who, having been summoned, have not entered easily. I urge you not to weaken yourselves.

In a tensed tempo of labor there is concealed a remarkable occult quality. No tension of the will whatsoever can yield the results attainable through strenuous labor. The tempo and saturation of rhythm can coalesce with cosmic tension.

350. You have already heard about the saturation of rhythm of labor as a particular quality possessed but rarely by people. Its beneficial influence has a far deeper significance than it may appear to have. Yet the ancient mysteries used these two expressions: "to labor in the wave of Sublime Nature" and "to work with the heartbeat of the Mother of the World."

Those who have studied profound subjects must

have known this labor of saturated rhythm, so that nothing could hinder them. The Teacher Buddha took much care that His disciples should know about changes of rhythm. Before great attainments He advised not repose but labor of saturated rhythm. Keep this in mind.

Among the problems of future evolution, remember that after solitary work it is necessary to pass to the organization of far more complex units.

One may have had occasion to see examples of the labor of saturated rhythm in separate individuals, or in very small communities, but a large crowd or assembly of people does not know how to utilize this principle.

There is an old saying—"Be cautious of the crowd." But there is another, equally old—"The crowd must be taught to work in spirit."

The external aspects of labor may be very diverse, but let rhythm be sensed and then the work will be of a completely different quality.

If the majority of contemporary families were not nurseries of vulgarity, then precisely they could be the guides to work united in spirit. But mechanical mothers and fathers know only how to chirp, "Do as everyone else does!"

Teach children to build their own cities.

351. About manuscripts.

The significance of manuscript has been completely forgotten.

Even the simplest physician understands that infection can be transmitted on a small piece of paper.

Pious kings and most holy cardinals have more than once used this to enhance their prosperity. Likewise, you know the experiments of contemporary hypnotists wherein at a command sealed letters are read. Even in circuses this exhibition is offered without additional charge.

This means that both the outer and inner significance of handwriting is important.

With one rubbing of the hand it is possible to cause little cork figures to leap up. Think how much energy may be impressed upon a sheet of paper through cooperation of the nerve centers.

One can observe the radiation of energy from the fingertips. In darkness these flashings can be seen. When the emanations are especially strong one can see even in daytime a blue light. Together with the radiation there is stratified on the paper an ineradicable energy similar in influence to the word and thought.

The writing carries not only the conventional connotation of the words used, but also a powerful communication of the human essence. From this point of understanding, one letter it may be preferable to hold in the hands, reading it over again, while another it is better not to touch at all. Of course, there are flying through the world many empty sheets of paper on which there has not remained a spark of the human consciousness.

How then is the difference to be understood? By spirit-knowledge, by that which decides where one can engage in handclasp.

Handwriting is a handshake at a distance.

352. It may be asked how the final Gates may be reached. We know the laws and signs; we waste no time; we remember to guard the Teaching; what shall we do if we find the Gates closed? For reply let us turn again to the Mysteries of ancient Egypt, as of course these Mysteries were scientific paths of life.

Without slackening the rhythm of his pace, the accepted candidate had to proceed to the Teacher. Before him stretched a luminous line and he had to follow it, not deviating nor brushing against it. The chambers through which he had to pass were lit by different colored fires. At times the line almost disappeared. But at last the line began to shine, and it was as if a dazzling ray passed on under a massive closed door. The door seemed to be impassable; it was without lock or handle. Bars and plates of various metals adorned and reinforced it.

The timid in spirit became disconcerted and upset the rhythm of the pace; but he who knew the significance of immutability went on resolutely. And when his body encountered the stronghold it fell to pieces, and he entered into the last chamber.

This irresistible impact of our earthly body is indispensable for the creation of the rhythm of ascent.

Spirit-knowledge indicates to us how the dimension of the goal governs the dimension of possibilities. The symbol of the heavy door falling to pieces exemplifies best of all how one should act.

Contemporary wiseacres ridicule breaking the wall with one's forehead, but the ancient Egyptians made a beautiful symbol of the power of our essential nature. Hence, proceed along the line of the ray.

Therefore, learn how to begin the new by assimilating the antecedent.

Be able to ignore derision directed at your courage, because you know whither you are going.

353. Again people will approach with the question as to how to deal with obstacles. Some are handicapped by family, some by distasteful occupation, some by poverty, some by attacks of enemies. But a good horseman likes to practice upon untrained horses, and prefers the obstacle of rough ground and ditches to a level roadway. Every impediment must be made the birth of a possibility. Disconcertion before an obstacle always emanates from fear. No matter how the cowardice be

garbed, We must reveal the page about fear. Friends, until impediments appear to us as the birth of possibilities, we will not understand the Teaching.

Success lies in expanded consciousness; it is impossible to approach it in fear. The ray of courage will lead above obstacles; because, as the world now knows, the seed of blood grows. The seed of knowledge grows, the seed of beauty grows!

If the path is strewn with bones, one can pass boldly; if people speak in different languages it means the soul can be revealed; if it is necessary to hasten, it means somewhere a new shelter is ready.

Blessed be the obstacles, through them we grow!

354. It can be justly asked how to treat animals. Usually either cruelty is employed toward them, or they are sentimentally made into parasites, or they are used as mediums for mechanical cross-breeding. Indeed a reasonable attitude toward animals must be established in accordance with the unity of world rhythm—this attitude is everywhere the same. Since man must be a coworker of evolution, animals too must conform to this law. Species which do not conform to evolution become extinct. Those adaptable to evolution must maintain their capacity for labor.

It is necessary to study the true usefulness of animals. It is vain to think that plesiosaurs are needed for the future. Grandmother's dress is very touching in a museum but poorly adapted to present-day life.

Successful progress of the world can be attained without the hippopotamus and the rhinoceros, who conformed very well to the former periods of strata deposits.

If a certain kind of men have a resemblance to the hippopotamus, then they are of the same evolution.

Animals must work, they must win the right to life;

hence, both cruelty and sentimentality are inapplicable. One cannot but love everything vitally laboring.

355. It being necessary for animals to labor, then how consciously must human toil be applied! Let us not differentiate between labors. The only distinction is between consciousness and senselessness. It is necessary to discern also the difference in age of the spirit. One can identify a recent spirit as compared with an old spirit by noting the difference in striving. A recent spirit does not have the deep perceptions that are inculcated by the experience of many lives, but often it has less egotism and is more adaptable to evolution.

An old spirit sometimes takes on the similitude of a funnel which draws the all-existent "I" into transformation by the personal ego. When such an abscess has formed, the sole cure is through achievement.

Beautiful and brilliant achievement promotes the regeneration of the subtle body. So long as such an old spirit strives for achievement, it still has vital capacity.

Since there is such a thing as gangrene of the body, there is also gangrene of the spirit. A dead limb can be removed in time, but gangrene of the spirit can be removed only by shock.

The spark of the blow gives birth to achievement. Of course, that achievement is preferable which grows consciously, when all one's being knows that the Teacher of Light does exist.

We knew a little girl in whom this knowledge immutably flashed out. Even sickness could not destroy this spirit-knowledge. Its forms were refracted, but the essence remained steadfast.

Thus, extend the essence into Infinity.

356. What external condition is indispensable for quality of labor? Light. Only light makes labor productive and useful. The butterfly can fly until its

rainbow pollen is exhausted. Man has the same rainbow force, which absorbs the power of the light by means of photoplasm. The different plasms are intermediaries between the visible and the invisible. Photoplasm, being an emanation of the nervous system, forms a rainbow pollen which absorbs rays of light and conveys them into the nerve channels.

The best connections with the light are obtained in the morning. Therefore, do not shut out the morning light. Work in the light, make decisions in the light, pass judgments in the light, grieve in the light, rejoice in the light. Nothing is to be compared with the light wave. Even the best electricity, even the bluest, yields eight thousand times less light than a ray of the sun.

Soon the study of photoplasm will give a new direction to methods of labor. One may see how the pollen of photoplasm effervesces, and how by tiny whirls it carries the received treasure into the pores of the skin.

Not only the problem of a spaciousness of workrooms but also that of a proper access for light must be studied.

The sun's rays must be appreciated as a world treasure.

The scientist will easily analyze the flow of rays from the other luminaries.

Why should people shun the treasures of the universe ordained for them?

Magnetic vortices of light constitute the rhythm of the planets. Cannot they be made use of, as is the power of the waterfall? Inexhaustible are the allotted forces.

John of the hundred-thousands, take your share! Soon, when endeavor turns into victory, the seed of the Common Good will give each one the power of the ray.

Thus let us remember when beginning the morning labor and courageously continuing it on into Infinity.

357. It is especially difficult for humanity to understand the relationship between quality of labor and infinity. The average man assumes that a higher quality of labor leads to the finite. For him quality is inextricable from finiteness, which We call deadliness. It is quite impossible to explain to the average man that higher quality aspires on into infinity. Precisely in the endlessness of higher tension lies the discovery of knowledge. One must find courage to labor for Infinity.

One can develop within oneself a continual learning, which is important not as a cataloguing of facts but as an expansion of consciousness.

It is not important by what means the consciousness grows, but its volume enables it to assimilate the scope of great events.

What teaching leads more swiftly to the broadening of consciousness? It is necessary to admit people completely individually to this meadow. To each one his own herbage, provided the inner fire conforms to human merit and dignity. The sluggish, the conceited, and those raging with suspicion and doubt will not find any nourishment.

Tell pupils and friends that they must learn. Let them learn in tension of the spirit; learn through opened eyes; learn absolutely endlessly, for there is no end. This simple affirmation fills many with terror.

But We are with those who say that there is light unto infinity and that whole eons glow like a string of pearls.

In learning let us not belittle.

358. Upon assembling the pupils, consider what to begin with. The usual mistake is to begin with the alphabet, disregarding the nature of the student. It is Our rule to give, along with the primary proposition, fragments of the highest possibilities.

Likewise, there must not be forgotten the favorite game of Buddha with His disciples in moments of relaxation, wherein the Teacher threw into space a single word upon which the disciples constructed an entire thought. There is no wiser test of the state of consciousness.

Picture it this way: The Teacher says, "Death," having in mind the death of vulgarity. Yet a disciple may exclaim, "Death to the poor!" Like guide-posts, such single words can weave a complete design of the spirit, and according to this pattern one can see what sort of fires are burning.

Such a case gives occasion to say, "Your consciousness desired death to the poor; therefore the riches directed to you have departed." Along with this primitive law one can launch a spark about the evolution of distant worlds. The comparison of the evolution of worlds with a small everyday matter can produce an enlightening stroke.

It is most difficult when a student wishes to cultivate the spirit by means of methodology. He may open a business for glossy paper advertisements, and sit, tapping with his pencil, enumerating the slogans not yet used.

We are not organizers of funeral processions or of zoological gardens. You who wish to follow Us, walk as fully and luminously imbued as irrestible life itself; and love every expansion of consciousness, because this is the primary aim.

One can forgive everything, but mouldiness of consciousness is worse than the decomposition of a corpse.

359. Even in children's periodicals, photographs of known persons are placed and along with them there may be discerned faces unfamiliar to anyone. Even a mechanical plate takes in more than the eye. And

perhaps this is better, for people do not trust their eyes but are full of respect for the photographic plate.

Astral guests crowd into the midst of life without attention being paid to them. Of course, it is not always easy for them to reach different people, and then one's earthly visitors serve as their mediators. Communication encounters difficulty, but the emanations of auras left by visitors or servants constitute a bridge for the invisible guests. The merit of these is very diverse—from the touch of a butterfly to the jaws of a tiger. Therefore, it is more practical to admit fewer people into your sleeping chambers and your workroom, if your own aura is already sufficiently steady.

Especially dangerous are the educators of children who come in with most horrible companions. The best sendings are often paralyzed by the presence of children's nursemaids and nurses. Therefore, self-activity is always useful. And again it is necessary to pay attention to secretaries, as they have ruined so many affairs.

Do things for yourself, and you may rest tranquil as to the quality of your own emanations.

360. "Why for him and not for me?" Thus whispers envy after midnight. Thrust this viper out of your undertakings.

Growth of spirit does not tolerate compulsion. This explains the slow evolution of humanity. The spirit cannot be forced to grow. One cannot even coerce by unsolicited counsels. One can only respond to the knock of a sensitive heart.

If you send the most obvious advice, that envy ruins the health, there will be evoked merely a new hypocrisy if there be no realization of the spirit.

But the paths of individual growth of spirit will be flooded with light.

Every drop of the ocean produces its own rainbow.

Hence, how beautiful is the radiance of the Cosmos! Therefore one must give replies carefully, because they are intended for an individual spirit.

We have spoken against present-day churches, yet it is inadmissible to speak against the clergy in toto. We knew an excellent Roman Catholic priest, but instead of being given a cardinalship he was transferred to a most wretched parish. We knew an exalted rabbi, but people considered him insane. We knew an enlightened Orthodox priest, but his lot was banishment to a distant monastery. I know of a cultured bishop in America but his life is not an easy one.

Each thought about the Common Good is persecuted unmercifully, whereas only growth of the individual spirit can fill the treasury of the General Welfare. This conformity of the individual spirit with the world Common Weal also constitutes the Beauty of the Cosmos.

If each plant has its own irreplaceable individuality, then how particularly must each human spirit be dealt with. Such tremor of sensitiveness must be a sign of Our disciples, and then without a word, through a simple contact, can light be shed.

And not only by day but also by night one can be in contact and can bring the help of enlightenment.

Be illumined through expansion of consciousness. As voyagers afar, accumulate knowledge through the rainbow pollen of the whole world.

361. Pure thoughts are like the ozone of space. Verily, one can fill one's surroundings with them, but only in a definite consonance. To launch a pure thought and muffle it with a dozen cravings is like a horrible dissonance. Consonance is to be understood as a series of resoundings in accord. Therefore, in self-activity We appreciate orderly sequence of actions. Not a chance benevolent exclamation,

but the conscious process of continuity produces advantages.

A parrot once knew how to screech, "Blessed Teacher!"—but by this it did not improve its possibilities. A bear chanced to leave its prey on the doorstep of a starving man, but it did not cease to be a wild animal. A bee accidentally pierced the abscess of a sick man, but it earned thereby no bliss for itself. Even a snake once saved a life by its poison. Only consciousness and staunchness yield results.

Consider the smile of achievement easy. And achievement which grows out of staunchness shines as a bountiful sun. Since the sweetness of a fruit does not depend upon its skin, let your activity proceed beyond the crowd. Only by avoiding crowds will you reach the people.

I can visualize a present-day minister of state or a Roman Pontiff driving up to Our Towers in a motor-car! Is there more of comedy or of tragedy here? In any case, a simple Mongol will be found to behave with more dignity, for in him the nerve of receptiveness has not been ruptured.

Friends, preserve a pure channel of receptivity, for in this furnace pure thoughts are forged. Look upon pure thoughts not as a wondrous Heaven-Dweller who descends on holidays, but as the fare of your workdays.

362. The first book summoned to attainment of beauty, simplicity, and fearlessness. The second gives the quality and the features of labor which affirm the expansion of consciousness.

The idea of the Community and of the Common Good is the first sign of broadening of consciousness. It should be understood that the necessity of labor is pointed out not for mere information but for application.

This book is not for soothing but for the exertion of the rising spirit. Strive to the utmost toward labor. Enwrap each task with the best emanation.

He who performs the most wearisome labor most joyously will be the resolute victor, for he overcomes the burden of boredom. Of course every path, even the path to Our Community, has difficult crossings. The scope of consciousness is measured not through the flowers but across the abyss.

The labor of endless perfectionment is ordained by Us. And in moments of difficulty think about Us, knowing that the wireless apparatus will not delay in connecting you with Us. But learn to think and to distinguish the moment of real difficulty. Often people take good fortune for calamity, and vice versa. Expansion of consciousness will affirm spirit-knowledge, and this knowledge will lead to Our Community.

Will there be a third book? Certainly there will, when the labor indicated in the second is brought into life. The third book must concern itself with Our Community. But can one speak about It, if the consciousness fails to assimilate the concept of community altogether?

Therefore, if you wish to manifest Our Community in life, you must first make manifest your own community. We will help you.

Observe without prejudices the course of world events and you will see Our Hand.

The time has drawn near for a turn in evolution, and forces for it have been gathered.

Learn to apply your best efforts, and in this labor accept Our greetings.

Welcome to all seekers of the Common Good.

AGNI YOGA SERIES

Agni Yoga Society
www.agniyoga.org

CPSIA information can be obtained
at www.ICGtesting.com
Printed in the USA
LVHW041844011219
639064LV00013B/750/P

9 781946 742414